# ·SPIKED·

## Desserts

Raspberry & Chocolate Shot, page 90.

# ·SPIKED·
# Desserts

## 75 Booze-Infused Party Recipes

**FOX CHAPEL**
PUBLISHING

ISBN 978-1-56523-722-3

Publisher's Cataloging-in-Publication Data

Spiked desserts : 75 booze-infused party recipes. -- East Petersburg, PA : Fox Chapel Publishing, c2012.

p. ; cm.

Includes index.

ISBN: 978-1-56523-722-3
Originally published as three separate titles (Drunken desserts, Shotcicles, and Booze-infused cakes) by CQ Products in 2010.
Summary: 75 recipes to bake or freeze alcohol-infused desserts, pops, and drinks.

1. Cooking (Liquors) 2. Cooking (Wine) 3. Desserts. 4. Frozen desserts. 5. Alcoholic beverages. 6. Cocktails.

TX726 .S65 2012

641.6/2--dc23

2012

To learn more about the other great books from Fox Chapel Publishing,
or to find a retailer near you, call toll-free 800-457-9112 or visit us at
www.FoxChapelPublishing.com.

**Note to Authors:** We are always looking for talented authors to write new books
in our area of cooking, woodworking, and crafts. Please send a brief letter
describing your idea to Acquisition Editor, 1970 Broad Street, East Petersburg, PA 17520.

Printed in China
First printing

Grown-Up S'Mores, page 78.

Bombsicle Ice, page 112.

# Introduction

Welcome to Spiked Desserts! Come in and make yourself a drink . . . and a drink-inspired dessert. If you've never concocted a delicious dessert with alcohol, you're in for some fun! The first section contains recipes for booze-infused cakes, cupcakes, and treats. Tapping into the inspiring flavor combinations of your favorite mixed drinks and shots opens a whole new world in your oven. Next time you host a cocktail party, wow your guests with Grasshopper Cupcakes (page 20), Fuzzy Navel Chiffon Cake (page 42), Pear Martini Crisp (page 60), and more. The second section contains recipes for shot-sicles and other frozen treats just perfect for those sizzling summer nights. Your freezer won't be the only thing chillin' when you mix up refreshing tipsy concoctions like Mudsicle Squares (page 96), Cosmo-Sicles (page 103), and Twisted Ice Cream Tiramisu (page 110). So mix up your favorite drink, pick a recipe, and let's get spiked!

Cheers!

Piña Colada Pops, page 97.

Grasshopper, page 120.

# Contents *Booze-Infused Cakes, Cupcakes & Treats*

Punchy Peach Fondue

Raspberry & Chocolate Shot

More Shots & Shooters

# Shot-sicles & Other Frozen Treats

Mango Pops

Piña Colada Pops

Mudsicle Squares

Mimosa Ice

Daiquiri Pops

Root Beer Pops

Cosmo-Sicles

B-52 Ice Cream Bomber

Just Peachy Bellini Pops

Choco-Sicles

'Root Beer' Slush

Cherry Vodka Granita

Twisted Ice Cream Tiramisu
110

Bombsicle Ice
112

Razzy Yo-Pops
113

Frozen Strawberry Margarita Pie
114

Punchy Pops
116

Lemon-Rum Creamsicles
117

Kiwi Colada
118

OJ-Gin Pops
119

Grasshopper
120

White Russian Granita
121

Lime-Pear Sorbet
122

Brandy Slush
123

Bombed Pops
124

Blasted Berries
125

Peppermint Shiver
126

# Booze-Infused Cakes, Cupcakes & Treats

## Tipsy Tips to Remember

Make guests aware of the alcoholic ingredients used in each dessert you serve.

Although heat from baking or simmering reduces the amount of booze in a cake or sauce, it does not get rid of all of it. The flavor remains, as does some of the alcohol (5 to 85%), so these cakes are not intended for consumption by children and others who wish to avoid liquor.

## Baking with Booze

○ When adding booze to cake batter, you may replace some of the required liquid in the recipe, but for best results, don't replace all of it.

○ Liquors may be used straight or stirred into a simple syrup made with equal parts sugar and water.

○ To stir booze into fillings or frostings, add it in small amounts to maintain correct texture. Taste often! To boost flavor, supplement the booze with complementary flavored extracts as needed.

○ Try poking holes into baked cake using a skewer, large fork or wooden spoon handle. Then gradually drizzle or brush booze over the top to add flavor and kick without over-soaking.

○ A flavor injector works well to infuse booze directly into baked, cooled cake.

○ For the biggest buzz, add alcohol to heated sauces or liquids after they have cooled to room temperature.

Chocolate Raspberry Cups, page 76.

# Drunken Strawberry Shortcake

Preheat oven to 325°. Line the bottom of an ungreased 9 x 9" baking pan with parchment paper; set aside. In a large bowl, combine strawberries with ¾ cup amaretto and ⅓ cup sugar; let berries soak at least 30 minutes. In a large mixing bowl, beat egg yolks on high speed until very thick and lemon-colored. Reduce speed to medium and gradually beat in ⅔ cup sugar. Add 3 tablespoons water and vanilla; mix well. Beat in flour; set aside. In a small mixing bowl with clean beaters, beat egg whites until frothy. Add cream of tartar and salt. Beat until whites are stiff but not dry. Fold beaten egg whites into yolk mixture. Spread batter in prepared pan and bake for 22 to 25 minutes or until cake tests done with a toothpick. Cool in pan.

In a small chilled mixing bowl with chilled beaters, beat whipping cream and remaining 2 tablespoons sugar until soft peaks form.  Fold in remaining 3 tablespoons amaretto (or less  to taste). Cut cake into 16 squares. Place one square on each serving plate and spoon strawberries and juice evenly over cake, using half the berries. Top with another cake square and spoon remaining strawberries and juice over the cake. Add a dollop of whipped cream on top before serving.

**Serves 8**

## You Will Need:

- ○ 6 C. sliced fresh strawberries
- ○ ¾ C. plus 3 T. amaretto, divided
- ○ 1 C. plus 2 T. sugar, divided
- ○ 4 eggs, separated
- ○ ¾ tsp. vanilla or almond extract
- ○ ¾ C. flour
- ○ ¼ tsp. cream of tartar
- ○ ⅛ tsp. salt
- ○ 1 C. heavy whipping cream

7 ½ oz. alcohol

# Harvey Wallbanger Cupcakes

Preheat oven to 350°. Line standard and/or mini muffin cups with paper liners; set aside. In a large mixing bowl, combine cake mix, pudding mix, oil, ½ cup orange juice, ⅓ cup Galliano, eggs, vodka and 1 teaspoon orange zest. Blend on low speed until moistened. Increase speed to medium and beat for 2 minutes more. Spoon batter into prepared pans, filling cups about ¾ full. Bake standard cupcakes for 12 to 16 minutes or mini cupcakes for 7 to 10 minutes or until cupcakes test done with a toothpick. Cool cupcakes in pan for 5 minutes before removing to a wire rack to cool completely.

Meanwhile, in a large mixing bowl, combine butter and remaining 1 teaspoon orange zest. Blend on low speed. Add powdered sugar, remaining 2½ tablespoons orange juice and remaining 1½ tablespoons Galliano. Beat on low speed until well mixed. Increase speed to medium and beat until frosting is light and fluffy. Pipe or spread frosting evenly on cupcakes.

**Serves 18**

## You Will Need:

- ○ 1 (18.25 oz.) pkg. orange cake mix
- ○ 1 (3.4 oz.) pkg. vanilla instant pudding mix
- ○ ½ C. vegetable oil
- ○ ½ C. plus 2½ T. orange juice, divided
- ○ ⅓ C. plus 1½ T. Galliano, divided
- ○ 4 eggs
- ○ 2 T. vodka
- ○ 2 tsp. orange zest, divided
- ○ ½ C. butter, softened
- ○ 3 C. powdered sugar, sifted

4½ oz. alcohol

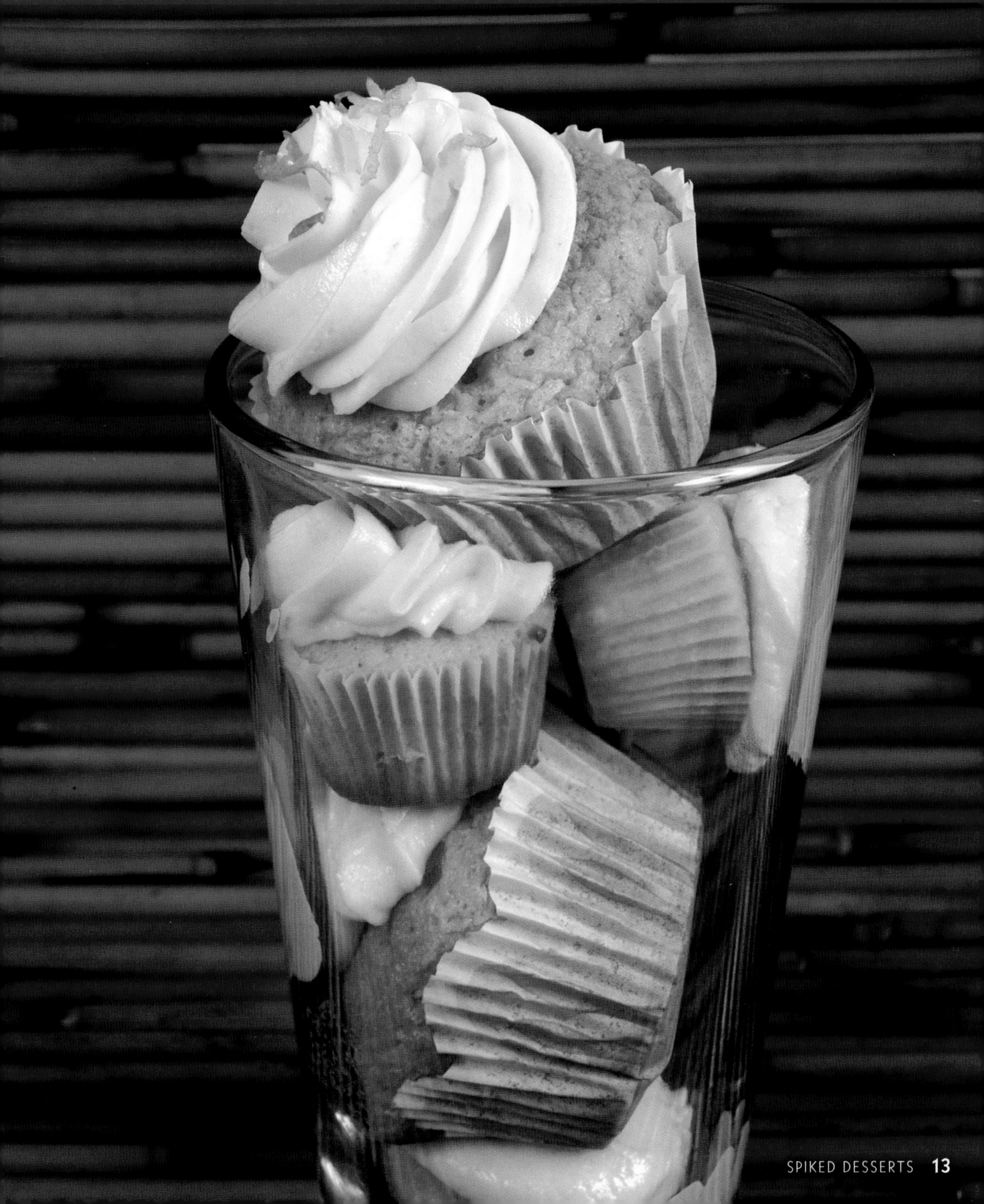

# Mai Tai Cheesecake

Preheat oven to 350°. Grease a 9" springform pan with nonstick cooking spray; set aside. In a small bowl, stir together coconut and butter until well combined. Press mixture into the bottom of prepared pan. Bake for 12 to 15 minutes or until golden brown. Let cool.

In a large mixing bowl, combine cream cheese, sugar and 5 teaspoons cornstarch. Beat on medium speed until smooth. Add eggs and egg yolk, one at a time, beating well after each addition. Reduce speed to low and beat in ⅓ cup orange juice concentrate, ¼ cup grenadine, ¼ cup triple sec, ¼ cup rum and vanilla until blended. Pour filling over crust. Bake for 15 minutes. Lower oven temperature to 200° and bake for 70 to 80 minutes or until the center is almost set but still jiggles slightly. Remove from oven and cool for 1 hour. Chill uncovered overnight.

In a small saucepan over medium heat, stir together lime juice and remaining ½ cup orange juice concentrate, 4 teaspoons grenadine and 1 tablespoon cornstarch. Cook and stir constantly until glaze is thickened and bubbly. Cook 2 minutes more. Remove from heat. Whisk in remaining 1 tablespoon triple sec and 1 tablespoon rum.

Run a knife around the inside edge of the pan, wiping knife frequently. Remove pan sides. Cut cheesecake into wedges and drizzle with glaze.

## To Serve

Spike orange and lime slices and maraschino cherries in triple sec for 30 minutes. Drain well on paper towels. Garnish cheesecake wedges with the spiked fruit.

**Serves 14**

## You Will Need:

- ◯ 1¾ C. sweetened flaked coconut
- ◯ 3 T. butter, melted
- ◯ 3 (8 oz.) pkgs. cream cheese, softened
- ◯ ¾ C. sugar
- ◯ 5 tsp. plus 1 T. cornstarch, divided
- ◯ 4 eggs
- ◯ 1 egg yolk
- ◯ ⅓ C. plus ½ C. frozen orange juice concentrate, thawed, divided
- ◯ ¼ C. plus 4 tsp. grenadine syrup, divided
- ◯ ¼ C. plus 1 T. triple sec, divided
- ◯ ¼ C. plus 1 T. light rum
- ◯ 2 tsp. clear vanilla extract
- ◯ 4 tsp. lime juice

5 oz. alcohol

# Chocolate Martini Swirls

Preheat oven to 350°. Lightly grease the bottom of a 10½ x 15½" jelly roll pan; set aside. In a medium bowl, combine brownie mix, eggs, oil, 2 tablespoons water and 2 tablespoons crème de cacao. Stir 50 strokes or until well blended. Spread batter in prepared pan. Bake for 15 to 19 minutes or until brownies test done with a toothpick. Let brownies cool completely in pan.

Empty both packages of pudding mix into a medium bowl. Add milk and whisk well until smooth and thickened, about 2 minutes. In a separate bowl, stir together vanilla vodka, chocolate liqueur and remaining 2 tablespoons crème de cacao. Add vodka mixture to pudding and whisk until well blended; set aside.

Cut out brownie rounds using three round cookie cutters in graduated sizes. For 8-ounce martini glasses, cut out five 1¾" rounds, five 2½" rounds and five 3¾" rounds. (Adjust brownie sizes for glass size.)

To assemble, put a spoonful of pudding mixture in the bottom of each martini glass. Set the smallest brownie round on pudding, pressing one edge down so brownie rests in glass at an angle. Spoon a layer of pudding on top of brownie. Set a medium brownie round on pudding at the same angle as first brownie. Add more pudding and top with the largest brownie round. Spread a level layer of pudding over the top. Sprinkle with chocolate curls. "Martinis" may be chilled before serving with spoons.

**Serves 5**

## You Will Need:

- ○ 1 (19 to 22 oz.) pkg. milk chocolate brownie mix
- ○ 2 eggs
- ○ ½ C. vegetable oil
- ○ 4 T. white crème de cacao, divided
- ○ 2 (3 oz.) pkgs. white chocolate instant pudding mix
- ○ 3 C. milk
- ○ ½ C. vanilla vodka
- ○ 2 T. chocolate cream liqueur
- ○ Chocolate curls*

7 oz. alcohol

* To make thick chocolate curls, rub a large milk chocolate candy bar against a grater to shave off curls of chocolate.

# Cosmopolitan Caketail

Soak half the cranberries in 2 tablespoons triple sec and the other half in 2 tablespoons vodka for 1 hour. Then drain off half the liquid. (Be sure to taste-test the drained liquid several times before discarding it!)

Preheat oven to 350°. Spray a 9 x 13" baking pan with nonstick cooking spray; set aside. In a large mixing bowl, beat together ½ cup butter and sugar until fluffy. Add eggs, one at a time, and beat until well combined. In a medium bowl, stir together flour, salt and baking powder. In a separate bowl, mix together buttermilk, ¾ cup cranberry juice concentrate, lime zest and soaked cranberries with remaining liquid. Add dry ingredients and wet ingredients alternately to butter mixture and beat on low speed until well mixed. Spread mixture evenly in prepared pan and bake for 35 to 45 minutes or until cake tests done with a toothpick. Cool cake for about 20 minutes in pan.

In a small bowl, stir together remaining ¼ cup cranberry juice concentrate and ¼ cup vodka; brush over warm cake. Cool completely.

In a large mixing bowl, beat together remaining ½ cup butter, lime juice (about ¼ cup), remaining 3 tablespoons triple sec and powdered sugar until light and fluffy. Cut cake and pipe frosting on each piece. Garnish with additional dried cranberries.

## You Will Need:

- 1 C. dried cranberries, chopped, plus more for garnish
- 5 T. triple sec, divided
- 2 T. plus ¼ C. vodka, divided
- 1 C. butter, softened, divided
- 2 C. sugar
- 2 eggs, room temperature
- 3 C. flour
- ½ tsp. salt
- 2½ tsp. baking powder
- ¾ C. buttermilk
- 1 C. frozen cranberry juice concentrate, thawed, divided
- Juice and zest from 1 lime
- 4 C. powdered sugar

5½ oz. alcohol

**Serves 20**

# Grasshopper Cupcakes

Preheat oven to 350°. Line standard muffin cups with paper liners; set aside. In a medium bowl, stir together flour, baking powder, salt and baking soda; set aside. Melt white chocolate in the microwave, stirring until smooth; set aside. In a large mixing bowl, cream butter on medium speed. Add sugar and beat until light and fluffy. Add eggs, one at a time, beating well after each addition. Reduce speed to low and mix in vanilla and melted chocolate. Add flour mixture and sour cream alternately to the creamed mixture, beating until just combined. Divide batter evenly between two bowls. Into one bowl, stir 3 tablespoons crème de menthe, mint flavoring and a little green food coloring, if desired. Into remaining bowl, stir 3 tablespoons crème de cacao. Use one spoonful of green batter and one spoonful of white batter side by side to fill each cupcake liner ²/₃ full. Bake for 16 to 19 minutes or until cupcakes test done with a toothpick. Cool completely.

Spoon frosting into a medium bowl. Add remaining 2 tablespoons crème de menthe and 2 tablespoons crème de cacao, stirring until well blended. Stir in yellow food coloring until frosting matches the green color in cupcakes. Dip the top of each cupcake into frosting, swirling to cover. Garnish with mint wedges and/or shavings.

**Serves 30**

## You Will Need:

- ○ 3 C. flour
- ○ 1 tsp. baking powder
- ○ ½ tsp. salt
- ○ ¼ tsp. baking soda
- ○ 4 (1 oz.) squares white baking chocolate
- ○ 1 C. butter, softened
- ○ 2 C. sugar
- ○ 4 eggs
- ○ 1 tsp. clear vanilla extract
- ○ ¾ C. sour cream
- ○ 5 T. green crème de menthe, divided
- ○ ½ tsp. mint flavoring
- ○ Green and yellow food coloring, optional
- ○ 5 T. white crème de cacao, divided
- ○ 1 (16 oz.) can whipped white frosting
- ○ Andes mints, wedges or shaved*

5 oz. alcohol

* To make mint wedges, cut each candy in half and then cut diagonally to make four wedges from each mint. To make shavings, slice the edge of a mint thinly with a vegetable peeler.

# Straight-Up Bourbon Balls

Melt chocolate chips in the microwave, stirring until smooth. Add cookie crumbs, plums, powdered sugar, bourbon and sweetened condensed milk. Stir until well combined. Cover and refrigerate for about 45 minutes.

Using 1 tablespoonful dough at a time, roll the mixture in your hands to create smooth, round balls. Store in an air-tight container at room temperature for 24 hours to allow flavors to combine.

Before serving, roll the balls in sugar to coat, if desired. Serve at room temperature. Refrigerate for up to a week or freeze for up to a month.

## To Serve

Layer several bourbon balls in brandy snifters to savor the aroma and enjoy them like fine liquor served straight-up.

## You Will Need:

**Serves 14**

- 1 C. semi-sweet chocolate chips
- 1½ C. finely crushed chocolate wafer cookies
- ½ C. finely chopped pitted dried plums
- ½ C. powdered sugar
- ¼ C. bourbon
- ¼ C. sweetened condensed milk
- ¼ C. sugar or colored decorating sugar, optional

2 oz. alcohol

# Dreamy Creamsicle Loaf

Preheat oven to 350°. Generously grease and flour two 5 x 9" loaf pans; set aside. In a small mixing bowl, beat together cake mix, egg white and orange juice. Stir in orange flavoring and orange food coloring as desired. Divide batter evenly between prepared pans. Bake for 12 to 14 minutes or until cakes test done with a toothpick. Let cool in pans for 15 minutes and then flip cakes out onto a wire rack to cool completely.

Soften ice cream in a large bowl. Line bottom and long sides of a clean loaf pan with parchment paper, allowing 2" to hang over long sides. If necessary, trim off the crown on both cakes. Set one cake layer in prepared pan. In a small bowl, stir together 1 tablespoon vanilla vodka and 1½ teaspoons triple sec. Brush half of the liquor mixture over the cake layer. Pour remaining 2 tablespoons vanilla vodka into softened ice cream and stir until smooth. Spread ice cream over cake in pan. Top with second cake layer and brush with remaining liquor mixture. Cover and freeze for 4 hours or overnight.

In a medium mixing bowl, beat together butter, vanilla, remaining 2½ tablespoons triple sec and powdered sugar until smooth and light. Dip bottom of loaf pan into warm water for 5 to 10 seconds and pull up on parchment paper to remove cake from pan. Set loaf and paper on a large plate. Spread frosting on sides and top of cake, working quickly. Sprinkle with orange sugar. Return to freezer for at least 1 hour. Remove parchment paper and set frozen loaf on a serving platter. Slice and serve cold.

## You Will Need:

Serves
10

- ○ 1 (9 oz.) pkg. white cake mix
- ○ 1 egg white
- ○ ½ C. orange juice
- ○ 1½ tsp. orange flavoring
- ○ Neon orange gel food coloring
- ○ 4 C. vanilla ice cream (white like Breyers)
- ○ 3 T. vanilla vodka, divided
- ○ 3 T. triple sec, divided
- ○ ½ C. butter, softened
- ○ 1½ tsp. vanilla extract
- ○ 3¾ C. powdered sugar, sifted
- ○ Orange decorating sugar

3 oz. alcohol

# Hot Buttered Rum Cake

Preheat oven to 325°. Grease and flour six 10- to 12-ounce mugs*. Melt ½ cup butter in the microwave. In a large mixing bowl, combine melted butter, cake mix, ice cream, eggs and buttermilk; beat on low speed until well blended. Fill each mug about ⅓ full with batter. Sprinkle batter with approximately half of the pecans and half of the brown sugar. Pour additional batter on top of brown sugar, filling mugs about ⅔ full. Sprinkle remaining pecans and brown sugar over the top of each. Bake for 35 to 40 minutes or until cakes test done with a toothpick. Cool completely.

In a small saucepan, melt remaining ½ cup butter, stirring constantly. Gradually add sugar and ¼ cup water; heat and stir constantly until well blended. Remove from heat and slowly stir in ½ cup rum. Using a large fork, carefully poke holes deeply into cakes. Slowly pour about ¼ cup rum mixture over cake in each mug, allowing it to soak into the cake.

In a small chilled mixing bowl with chilled beaters, whip cream with remaining 1 tablespoon rum and powdered sugar until soft peaks form. Top cakes with spiked whipped cream and sprinkle with cinnamon, if desired.

## You Will Need:

**Serves 6**

- 1 C. butter, divided
- 1 (18 oz.) pkg. butter pecan cake mix
- 1 pt. butter pecan ice cream, softened
- 4 eggs
- ½ C. buttermilk
- 1 C. crushed pecans, divided
- ¼ C. brown sugar, divided
- 1 C. sugar
- ½ C. plus 1 T. rum, divided
- ½ C. heavy whipping cream
- 2 T. powdered sugar
- Dash of cinnamon, optional

4½ oz. alcohol

* Be sure mugs are ovenproof. Cake can also be made in a greased and floured 12-cup Bundt pan. Bake for 1 hour.

# Hard Lemonade Layer Cake

Preheat oven to 350°. Grease and flour two 9" round baking pans; line bottoms with parchment paper and set aside. Separate yolks and whites of 6 eggs. In a medium bowl, whisk together flour, baking powder, baking soda and salt; set aside. In a large mixing bowl, beat ¾ cup butter. Gradually beat in 1½ cups sugar, then egg yolks, one at a time. Add 1 teaspoon vanilla; set aside. In a small bowl, combine buttermilk, cream of coconut and ¼ cup hard lemonade. Add flour and buttermilk mixtures alternately to the butter mixture, beating until blended; set aside. Using a clean mixing bowl and beaters, beat 6 egg whites until frothy. Add cream of tartar and beat until soft peaks form. Beat in ¼ cup sugar, until stiff glossy peaks form. Fold beaten egg whites into batter to blend. Divide batter between prepared pans. Bake for 35 to 40 minutes or until cakes test done with a toothpick. Let cool in pans for 10 minutes. Loosen edges and invert cakes onto a greased wire rack. Remove pans and turn cakes right side up; cool completely.

Combine lemon juice with enough hard lemonade to equal ⅓ cup liquid and place in the top of a double boiler. Whisk in 3 eggs and ¾ cup sugar. Cook over simmering water (pan should not touch water) and stir constantly for 10 to 20 minutes or until mixture thickens and reaches 160°. Remove from heat and strain out lumps. Cut up remaining ¼ cup butter and whisk into mixture until melted. Stir in lemon zest. Cover lemon curd and let cool. Refrigerate until chilled and thick.

Cut each cake layer in half horizontally. Place one layer on a serving plate. Spread with ⅓ of the chilled curd and 2½ tablespoons coconut. Repeat with two more layers of cake, curd and coconut, ending with cake on top.

In the top of a clean double boiler, combine 2 egg whites, remaining 1½ cups sugar, ¼ cup hard lemonade and corn syrup. Cook over simmering water and beat for 3 to 4 minutes on low speed. Increase speed and beat for 5 minutes or until frosting is shiny and smooth with soft peaks. Remove from heat and add remaining 1 teaspoon vanilla. Beat on high for 1 to 2 minutes or until thick. Immediately spread frosting over entire cake. Sprinkle with remaining 1 cup coconut. Cover and chill before serving.

## You Will Need:

**Serves 14**

- 9 eggs, room temperature, divided
- 2½ C. flour
- 2 tsp. baking powder
- ½ tsp. baking soda
- ¼ tsp. salt
- 1 C. butter, softened, divided
- 4 C. sugar, divided
- 2 tsp. vanilla extract, divided
- 1¼ C. buttermilk
- ¼ C. cream of coconut
- 1 (11.2 oz.) bottle hard lemonade
- 2 egg whites
- ½ tsp. cream of tartar
- Juice from 1 lemon (2 T.)
- 1 T. finely grated lemon zest
- 1½ C. sweetened flaked coconut, divided
- 1 T. light corn syrup

5½ oz. alcohol

# Mini Mountain Mudslides

Line 6 cavities of an ice cube tray with plastic wrap, pressing down firmly; set aside. Place dark chocolate in a glass measuring cup. Heat cream and corn syrup to a boil in the microwave, stirring several times. Pour hot cream mixture over chocolate, let stand for 30 seconds and whisk until smooth. Stir in 1 teaspoon Mudslide liqueur, 1½ teaspoons sugar and ½ teaspoon vanilla. Pour chocolate mixture evenly into prepared tray. Cover and freeze for 3 to 4 hours or until solid.

Preheat oven to 425°. Generously butter six 6-ounce ramekins and place on a baking sheet. Combine semi-sweet baking chocolate, 1 tablespoon sugar and remaining ¼ cup Mudslide liqueur and microwave until chocolate is softened; stir until smooth. Cool. In a small bowl, stir together flour and salt; set aside. In a medium mixing bowl, beat butter on medium speed until creamy. Gradually add ½ cup sugar and remaining 2 teaspoons vanilla, beating until light and fluffy. Add egg yolks, one at a time, beating well after each addition. Add cooled chocolate mixture and beat until smooth.

In a medium mixing bowl, use clean beaters to beat egg whites until soft peaks form. Gradually beat in remaining 1 tablespoon sugar until stiff glossy peaks form. Gently fold ⅓ of the beaten egg whites and ⅓ of the flour mixture into chocolate batter. Repeat until all egg whites and flour are incorporated. Divide half the batter evenly between prepared ramekins. Place one frozen chocolate cube in the center of each ramekin;

press down slightly. Spoon remaining batter over chocolate cubes to cover completely. Bake for 12 to 15 minutes or until edges test done with a toothpick. Do not overbake.

Invert warm cakes onto individual serving plates. Dust with powdered sugar or top with ice cream or whipped cream, if desired. Serve immediately.

## You Will Need:

**Serves 6**

- ¼ C. heavy whipping cream
- 1 T. light corn syrup
- 2 oz. dark chocolate, coarsely chopped
- 1 tsp. plus ¼ C. Mudslide liqueur, divided
- 2½ T. plus ½ C. sugar, divided
- 2½ tsp. vanilla extract, divided
- 8 (1 oz.) squares semi-sweet baking chocolate, coarsely chopped
- ¾ C. plus 3 T. flour, sifted
- ⅛ tsp. salt
- ½ C. butter, softened
- 3 egg yolks, room temperature
- 4 egg whites, room temperature
- Powdered sugar, vanilla ice cream or whipped cream, optional

2 oz. alcohol

# Mint Julep Cupcakes

Preheat oven to 325°. Line standard muffin cups with foil liners; set aside. In a medium mixing bowl, stir together flour, sugar, salt, baking powder and baking soda. Make a well in the center. In a separate bowl, combine buttermilk, eggs, vanilla, crème de menthe and 1 teaspoon mint extract, stir well. Add buttermilk mixture and melted butter to flour mixture. Beat on low speed until combined. Increase speed to medium and beat for 3 minutes more. Spoon batter into prepared pans, filling cups about ⅔ full. Bake for 18 to 20 minutes or until cupcakes test done with a toothpick.

Meanwhile, in a small saucepan over medium heat, stir together ½ cup powdered sugar, ⅓ cup butter and 2 tablespoons water until butter melts and mixture is blended. Do not boil. Remove from heat and stir for 2 minutes. Whisk in ¼ cup bourbon. When cupcakes are done, remove from oven and let cool slightly. With a fork, poke deep holes in the top of each cupcake. Drizzle some of the bourbon butter sauce over each cupcake, allowing it to fill holes. Repeat to use all sauce. Let cupcakes cool completely.

In a large mixing bowl, combine cream cheese, remaining 3½ cups powdered sugar, remaining 4 teaspoons bourbon and remaining ¼ teaspoon mint extract. Beat on medium speed until smooth and creamy. Spread or pipe frosting on cupcakes. Cut plastic straws into 4" lengths. Garnish cupcakes with mint leaves and insert straws to resemble small mint julep cocktails.

**Serves 16**

## You Will Need:

- 1½ C. cake flour
- 1 C. sugar
- ½ tsp. salt
- ½ tsp. baking powder
- ¼ tsp. baking soda
- 6 T. buttermilk
- 2 eggs, lightly beaten
- 1 tsp. vanilla extract
- 4 tsp. green crème de menthe
- 1¼ tsp. mint extract, divided
- ½ C. butter, melted
- 4 C. powdered sugar, divided
- ⅓ C. butter
- ¼ C. plus 4 tsp. bourbon, divided
- 1 (8 oz.) pkg. cream cheese, softened

3½ oz. alcohol

# Tequila Sunrise Bundt Cake

Preheat oven to 350°. Generously grease and flour a 9" Bundt pan and set aside. If desired, soak cherries in 2 tablespoons tequila. In a large mixing bowl, combine cake mix, eggs, oil, ¾ cup orange juice concentrate, orange flavoring and ½ cup tequila. Blend on low speed until moistened. Increase speed to medium and beat for 2 minutes. Divide batter evenly between three bowls (about 1½ cups per bowl). Leave one bowl plain. Add red food coloring to second bowl to achieve a medium orange color. Add more red food coloring to third bowl to achieve a dark red-orange color. Drain cherries and guzzle any extra tequila (if you must). Place cherries in bottom of prepared pan, setting one cherry in each groove. Carefully spoon the plain batter into pan, covering cherries. Spread orange batter over plain batter to cover. Top with red-orange batter. Bake for 30 to 35 minutes or until cake tests done with a toothpick.

Remove cake from oven. Drizzle grenadine over the top of hot cake. Let cool in pan for 10 minutes. Carefully invert cake onto a wire rack and remove pan. Whisk together remaining 1 tablespoon orange juice concentrate, remaining 1 tablespoon tequila and powdered sugar. Brush glaze over warm cake. Let cool completely. Slice cake into wedges to serve.

## You Will Need:

**Serves 14**

- Maraschino cherries (about 16), well drained
- 3 T. plus ½ C. golden tequila, divided
- 1 (18.25 oz.) pkg. yellow cake mix
- 3 eggs
- ⅓ C. vegetable oil
- ¾ C. plus 1 T. orange juice concentrate, thawed, divided
- 1 tsp. orange flavoring
- Red gel food coloring
- 3 to 5 T. grenadine syrup
- 1 T. powdered sugar, sifted

5½ oz. alcohol

# Pucker-Up Margaritas

In the top of a double boiler over medium-high heat, stir together 1 cup sugar, butter, ¾ cup lime juice and 1 tablespoon lime zest until butter melts. In a small bowl, whisk eggs with 2 tablespoons hot lime mixture. Reduce heat until water simmers. Slowly whisk egg mixture into lime mixture. Cook until lime curd thickens and coats the back of a wooden spoon, 10 to 20 minutes; cool. Stir in food coloring, if desired, and set aside.

In a small glass bowl, stir together triple sec and 1 tablespoon tequila; sprinkle with gelatin and let stand for 1 minute. Microwave on high for 20 to 30 seconds or until gelatin dissolves. In a medium bowl, stir together ⅓ cup lime juice, orange juice and 1 teaspoon lime zest. Whisk in gelatin mixture. Place ice and water into a larger bowl, deep enough so the bowl with gelatin mixture rests in the water but does not submerge. Place bowl with gelatin mixture into ice water and whisk in sour cream until smooth; let stand 15 to 20 minutes, whisking occasionally, until mixture thickens. Meanwhile, in a small chilled mixing bowl with chilled beaters, beat whipping cream until soft peaks form. Fold whipped cream into thickened gelatin mixture. Refrigerate several hours or until mousse mounds when dropped from a spoon.

To assemble, mix several spoonfuls of sugar with remaining lime zest on a small plate. Coat the rims of four margarita glasses with lime juice. Dip rims in sugar mixture, coating well. Divide lime curd evenly between glasses. Top each serving with one cake, hollow side facing up. Brush cakes with remaining 2 tablespoons tequila. Divide mousse mixture evenly between glasses, mounding it in the hollow of each cake. Garnish rims with a lime slice, if desired.

## You Will Need:

**Serves 4**

- 1⅓ C. sugar, divided
- ¼ C. butter
- ¾ C. plus ⅓ C. lime juice, divided
- Finely grated zest from 1 lime, divided
- 2 eggs, beaten
- Green food coloring, optional
- 1 T. triple sec
- 3 T. tequila, divided
- 1½ tsp. unflavored gelatin
- 2½ T. orange juice
- ⅓ C. sour cream
- ⅔ C. heavy whipping cream
- 4 purchased round shortcakes
- Lime slice, optional

2 oz. alcohol

# Toast to Champagne Cake

Preheat oven to 350°. Grease and flour two 8 x 8" baking pans; set aside. In a large mixing bowl, combine cake mix, egg whites, $^2/_3$ cup champagne and cherry juice; beat on medium speed for 4 minutes. Spread half of batter in each prepared pan. Bake for 20 to 25 minutes or until cakes test done with a toothpick. Remove from oven; let cool in pans for 10 minutes. Loosen edges of cakes. Invert and gently tap on pans to remove cakes; cool completely.

In a small chilled mixing bowl with chilled beaters, beat whipping cream on high speed until almost stiff; set aside. In a small mixing bowl, beat together shortening, remaining $^1/_3$ cup champagne, powdered sugar, salt and vanilla until well mixed. Remove ¼ cup of frosting and tint it with red food coloring to reach desired shade of pink; refrigerate until serving time. Place one cake on a serving plate, top side up. Spread half of the white frosting evenly over top of cake. Set remaining cake on frosted layer, top side up. Fold whipped cream into remaining white frosting and frost sides and top of cake. Refrigerate until ready to serve. At serving time, cut cake and pipe reserved pink frosting on each piece. Sprinkle with crushed candy, if desired.

## You Will Need:

**Serves 9**

- 1 (18.25 oz.) pkg. white cake mix
- 2 egg whites
- 1 C. dry champagne, divided
- $^2/_3$ C. maraschino cherry juice
- 1 C. heavy whipping cream
- $^1/_3$ C. vegetable shortening (white)
- 4¼ C. powdered sugar, sifted
- Pinch of salt
- 1 tsp. vanilla extract or cherry flavoring
- Red gel food coloring
- Coarsely crushed white or pink rock candy, optional

8 oz. alcohol

# Caramelicious Appletini Cupcakes

Preheat oven to 350°. Spray mini muffin pans with nonstick cooking spray; set aside. In a large bowl, whisk together flour, sugar, baking soda and salt; set aside. In a separate bowl, whisk together eggs, oil, apple cider, vodka, 2 tablespoons apple pucker, vanilla and applesauce until blended. Add egg mixture to dry ingredients and stir well. Stir in green food coloring as desired. Spoon batter into prepared pans, filling cups about ⅔ full. Bake for 7 to 8 minutes or until cupcakes test done with a toothpick. Let cool in pans for 5 minutes; remove to a wire rack to cool completely.

Pour 2 tablespoons apple pucker into a small bowl. Dip the top of each cupcake into the liquor and then dip into green sugar to coat; let dry on waxed paper. Meanwhile, in a small saucepan over low heat, melt butter. Add brown sugar and milk; cook and stir for 1 minute or until sugar melts. Remove from heat and cool slightly. In a medium bowl, combine butter mixture, 2 teaspoons apple pucker and 1 teaspoon butterscotch schnapps. Gradually add powdered sugar and beat until smooth. Beat in more apple pucker and butterscotch schnapps as needed, 1 teaspoon at a time, to reach a smooth piping consistency; set aside.

In a small saucepan over medium heat, combine half & half and caramels. Cook and stir until melted and smooth. Cool to room temperature.

## To Serve

Stack 4 mini cupcakes in each martini glass. Pipe frosting on top and drizzle with caramel sauce.

**Serves 14**

## You Will Need:

- ○  2 C. flour
- ○  ½ C. sugar
- ○  1 tsp. baking soda
- ○  ¼ tsp. salt
- ○  2 eggs, lightly beaten
- ○  ½ C. vegetable oil
- ○  2 T. apple cider or juice
- ○  2 T. vodka
- ○  ¼ C. plus 3 tsp. sour apple pucker schnapps, divided
- ○  1 tsp. vanilla extract
- ○  1 C. Granny Smith applesauce
- ○  Green food coloring, optional
- ○  Green decorating sugar
- ○  2 T. butter
- ○  ¼ C. dark brown sugar
- ○  2 T. milk
- ○  2 tsp. butterscotch schnapps, divided
- ○  2 C. powdered sugar, sifted
- ○  ¼ C. half & half
- ○  15 caramels, unwrapped

4 oz. alcohol

# Fuzzy Navel Chiffon Cake

Remove one oven rack and place remaining rack in the bottom third of oven. Preheat oven to 350°. In a large bowl, whisk together cake flour, ¾ cup sugar, baking powder and ½ teaspoon salt; set aside. In a separate bowl, whisk egg yolks, orange zest, orange juice, ½ cup peach schnapps and oil. Pour juice mixture over dry ingredients and whisk just until smooth; set aside. In a large bowl, beat 8 egg whites until frothy. Add cream of tartar and beat on high speed until soft peaks form. Gradually add remaining ¾ cup sugar, beating until stiff glossy peaks form. Fold ¼ of beaten egg whites into batter until just blended. Gently fold in remaining egg whites. Spread batter in an ungreased 10" angel food cake pan. Run a spatula through batter to eliminate any large air bubbles; smooth top. Bake for 40 minutes or until cake springs back when lightly touched. Remove pan from oven and immediately turn upside down on pan legs or a tall bottle. Let cool completely. Run a knife around inside of pan and center tube. Invert cake onto a large serving plate and remove pan.

In a large mixing bowl, cream butter and shortening on medium speed until light and fluffy, about 10 minutes. Add powdered sugar and beat until blended. Add remaining 2 tablespoons peach schnapps, triple sec, vanilla, remaining ¼ teaspoon salt and cream; blend on low speed. Increase speed and beat until light and fluffy, about 5 minutes. Blend in a small amount of red and yellow food coloring to make light orange. Spread frosting over entire cake. Sprinkle with orange sugar, if desired. Garnish with sliced peaches or oranges. Chill before serving.

Soak sliced peaches in peach schnapps and/or sliced oranges in triple sec. Drain well before garnishing cake.

## You Will Need:

- 2¼ C. sifted cake flour
- 1½ C. sugar, divided
- 1 T. baking powder
- ¾ tsp. salt, divided
- 6 eggs, separated, room temperature
- 2 T. finely grated orange zest
- ¼ C. orange juice
- ½ C. plus 2 T. peach schnapps, divided
- ½ C. vegetable oil
- 2 egg whites
- ½ tsp. cream of tartar
- ½ C. heavy whipping cream
- 2 T. triple sec
- ½ C. butter, softened
- ½ C. vegetable shortening (white)
- 4 C. powdered sugar
- 1 tsp. vanilla extract
- Orange decorating sugar, optional
- Spiked sliced peaches and/or oranges

6 oz. alcohol

**Serves 16**

# After-Dinner Drink Cupcakes

Preheat oven to 350°. Line standard muffin cups with paper liners; set aside. In a large mixing bowl, combine cake mix, buttermilk, oil and eggs. Blend on low speed until moistened. Increase speed and beat for 2 minutes. Spoon batter into prepared pans, filling cups about ²/₃ full. Bake for 15 to 20 minutes or until cupcakes test done with a toothpick. Let cool in pans for 10 minutes; remove to cool completely. (To make Peppermint Patties, set a chocolate patty on six warm cupcakes to soften; spread over cupcakes and let cool.)

In a medium mixing bowl, beat together shortening, sugar, vanilla, milk, salt and 2 teaspoons water for 7 to 8 minutes. Add powdered sugar and beat until light and fluffy, about 5 minutes. Divide filling between four bowls. Add 1 to 2 teaspoons of one liquor mixture (listed at the right) to each bowl; mix and set aside. Fill injector with one of the remaining liquor mixtures. Poke the needle into a cupcake several times, avoiding the center, and inject up to 5 ml. of liquor into six cupcakes. Refill injector as needed. Repeat to make six cupcakes of each flavor. Let stand for 20 to 30 minutes.

Using a pastry bag fitted with a long piping tip, pipe filling into like-flavored cupcakes, finishing tops with a swirl of filling. Make six cupcakes of each flavor.

## Peppermint Patty

Mix 1 tablespoon crème de cacao with 2 tablespoons peppermint schnapps. Unwrap 6 chocolate peppermint patties; set aside.

## Golden Cadillac

Mix 1 tablespoon Galliano and 1½ tablespoons white crème de cacao.

## Brandy Alexander

Mix 4 teaspoons brandy with 4 teaspoons dark crème de cacao.

## Pink Squirrel

Mix 4 teaspoons crème de almond and 4 teaspoons white crème de cacao.

### You Will Need:

- 1 (18.25 oz.) pkg. French vanilla cake mix
- 1 C. buttermilk
- ⅓ C. vegetable oil
- 4 eggs
- 1⅓ C. vegetable shortening (white)
- 1 C. sugar
- 2 tsp. vanilla extract
- ⅔ C. milk
- ½ tsp. salt
- 2 C. powdered sugar
- Approximately 3 T. liquor mixture of each flavor (for every 6 cupcakes)

6 oz. alcohol

**Serves 24**

# Singapore Sling Trifle

Preheat oven to 350°. Spray a 10½ x 15½" jelly roll pan with nonstick cooking spray. In a large mixing bowl, combine cake mix, oil, eggs, club soda and gin. Beat on medium speed until well blended, about 2 minutes. Spread batter evenly in prepared pan. Bake for 10 to 14 minutes or until cake tests done with a toothpick. Let cool completely in pan.

Meanwhile, in a medium bowl, whisk together pudding mix, milk and cherry brandy for 2 minutes or until well combined and thickened. Cover and refrigerate until ready to assemble.

When cool, cut cake into about 100 (¾") cubes*. Place four or five cake cubes in each 10-ounce Collins glass. If desired, drizzle cake with ¼ teaspoon cherry brandy. Follow with approximately 2 tablespoons pie filling and 2 tablespoons pudding for each serving. Repeat layers of cake, cherry brandy, pie filling and pudding. Top with a few cake cubes and a maraschino cherry.

* Note: You will have extra cake.

**Serves 8**

## You Will Need:

- 1 (18.25 oz.) pkg. lemon cake mix (pudding type)
- Vegetable oil and eggs as directed on cake mix package
- ¾ C. club soda
- ¼ C. gin
- 1 (3 oz.) pkg. vanilla instant pudding mix
- 1½ C. milk
- ½ C. cherry brandy, plus more for drizzling
- 1 (21 oz.) can cherry pie filling (or more to taste)
- Maraschino cherries

6 oz. alcohol

# Tootsie Cake Roll

Preheat oven to 350°. Line a 10½ x 15½" jelly roll pan with aluminum foil, extending foil 1" over pan edges. Grease and flour foil; set aside. Generously sprinkle cocoa powder and powdered sugar over a large tea towel; set aside. In a medium mixing bowl, beat egg yolks and ½ cup sugar until light, about 5 minutes. Melt 4 chocolate squares in the microwave, stirring until smooth; cool slightly. Stir chocolate into egg mixture. Add orange juice concentrate and orange flavoring, beating until smooth. In a small bowl, whisk together flour, baking powder, baking soda and ¼ teaspoon salt. Add flour mixture to chocolate mixture and beat until blended; set aside. In a large bowl using clean beaters, beat egg whites until frothy. Add cream of tartar and beat on high speed until soft peaks form. Gently fold chocolate mixture into egg whites until blended. Spread batter in prepared pan. Bake for 11 to 14 minutes or until cake tests done with a toothpick. Loosen sides of cake from foil. Immediately invert cake onto prepared towel. Peel off foil. Starting at a short end, roll up warm cake with towel inside, jelly roll fashion. Set on a wire rack to cool completely.

In a medium mixing bowl, beat butter until creamy. Melt remaining chocolate square; cool slightly, add to butter and beat well. Beat in dash of salt and ½ cup powdered sugar. Add 3 tablespoons crème de cacao and 3 tablespoons triple sec, beating on low speed until blended. Gradually beat in 1½ cups powdered sugar. Stir in whipped topping. Unroll cake and remove towel. Spread cake with filling, almost to edges. Re-roll cake without towel and freeze for at least 30 minutes.

Whisk together orange juice with remaining 2 tablespoons triple sec, 2 tablespoons crème de cacao, 1 cup powdered sugar and chocolate syrup, if desired. Slice cake and drizzle with orange sauce.

**Serves 10**

## You Will Need:

- ○ Unsweetened cocoa powder and powdered sugar for sprinkling
- ○ 3 eggs, separated
- ○ ½ C. plus 2 T. sugar, divided
- ○ 5 (1 oz.) squares semi-sweet baking chocolate, divided
- ○ ⅓ C. orange juice concentrate, thawed
- ○ 1 tsp. orange flavoring or vanilla extract
- ○ ¾ C. flour
- ○ 1 tsp. baking powder
- ○ ½ tsp. baking soda
- ○ ¼ tsp. plus dash of salt
- ○ ¼ tsp. cream of tartar
- ○ ¼ C. butter, softened
- ○ 3 C. powdered sugar, divided
- ○ 5 T. dark or white crème de cacao, divided
- ○ 5 T. triple sec, divided
- ○ ¾ C. whipped topping, thawed
- ○ 2 T. orange juice
- ○ ½ tsp. chocolate syrup, optional

5 oz. alcohol

# Strawberry Daiquiri Mini Cakes

Preheat oven to 350°. Grease and flour five 4" springform pans or 8 to 10 jumbo muffin cups; set aside. In a large mixing bowl, combine cake mix, eggs, ¾ cup daiquiri mix concentrate, ½ cup rum and oil; beat on medium speed for 2 minutes. Divide batter evenly between prepared pans. Bake mini cakes for 24 to 25 minutes and jumbo cupcakes for 18 to 20 minutes or until cakes test done with a toothpick.

Meanwhile, in a small saucepan over medium heat, whisk together ¼ cup sugar, lime juice and remaining ¼ cup daiquiri mix concentrate. Cook, stirring until sugar dissolves. Remove from heat, let cool slightly and stir in 1 tablespoon rum. Poke holes in warm cakes with a fork and brush the glaze over cake, letting it soak in. Cool completely on wire racks.

In the top of a double boiler, combine ¼ cup cold water, egg whites, cream of tartar, corn syrup, salt and remaining ½ cup sugar. Beat for 1 minute on medium speed. Place pan over boiling water (pan should not touch water) and beat on high speed for 7 minutes or until sugar dissolves and mixture reaches 160°. Remove pan from boiling water and add vanilla. Beat again until icing stands in stiff glossy peaks. Spread on cake and cut into wedges. Best when served the same day.

## Variation

Use homemade or ready-to-spread strawberry frosting or vanilla frosting with 2 tablespoons daiquiri mix or rum stirred in. If desired, sprinkle white sparkling sugar around the top edge of each cake.

**Serves 16**

## You Will Need:

- ○ 1 (18.25 oz.) pkg. strawberry cake mix
- ○ 3 eggs
- ○ 1 C. frozen strawberry daiquiri mix concentrate, thawed, divided
- ○ ½ C. plus 1 T. rum, divided
- ○ ⅓ C. vegetable oil
- ○ ¾ C. sugar, divided
- ○ 2½ T. lime juice
- ○ 2 egg whites, room temperature
- ○ ¼ tsp. cream of tartar
- ○ 1 T. light corn syrup
- ○ Dash of salt
- ○ 1 tsp. vanilla extract

4½ oz. alcohol

# Drunken Peach Pie Bars

Preheat oven to 400°. Lightly spray a 9 x 13" baking pan with nonstick cooking spray; set aside. In a medium bowl, stir together 2½ cups flour and 1 teaspoon salt. With a pastry blender or two knives, cut in shortening until crumbly; set aside. In a small bowl, beat 1 egg yolk (reserve egg white). Add 6 tablespoons plus 2 teaspoons milk and mix well; stir egg mixture into flour mixture until dough forms. On a floured surface, roll half the dough to a 13 x 15" rectangle. Carefully transfer dough to prepared pan and press firmly in the bottom and up the sides of pan. Sprinkle corn flakes over dough in bottom of pan.

In a large bowl, stir together brown sugar, 2 tablespoons flour, cornstarch, cinnamon and remaining ½ teaspoon salt. Add peaches and mix gently to combine; set aside.

In a separate small bowl, whisk together ½ cup peach schnapps, 1 whole egg and 1¼ teaspoons almond extract. Add to peach mixture and stir to combine. Spoon peach mixture into prepared pan. Trim bottom pastry even with the peaches.

On a floured surface, roll remaining dough to a 9 x 13" rectangle. Transfer dough to prepared pan, covering peach mixture and trimming edges to fit if necessary. Seal together edges of bottom and top pastries using a little water. Cut several small slits in top crust.

Whisk together reserved egg white and remaining 1 tablespoon milk until well blended. Brush top pastry with egg white mixture; sprinkle with coarse sugar.

Bake for 10 to 15 minutes; reduce heat to 375° and bake for 40 minutes more or until pastry is dark golden brown and filling is bubbly. Cool completely. Cut into bars.

In a small bowl, stir together powdered sugar, butter, remaining 2½ tablespoons peach schnapps and remaining ½ teaspoon almond extract, adding more schnapps if necessary until glaze is thin and smooth. Drizzle over bars as desired.

## You Will Need:

**Serves 12**

- ○ 2¾ C. flour, divided
- ○ 1½ tsp. salt, divided
- ○ 1 C. vegetable shortening
- ○ 2 eggs, divided
- ○ 7 T. plus 2 tsp. milk, divided
- ○ 1 C. corn flakes cereal
- ○ 1 C. brown sugar
- ○ 2 T. cornstarch
- ○ 1 tsp. ground cinnamon
- ○ 3 to 3½ lbs. ripe peaches, peeled, sliced
- ○ ½ C. plus 2½ T. peach schnapps, divided
- ○ 1¾ tsp. almond extract, divided
- ○ ¼ C. coarse sugar
- ○ 1¼ C. powdered sugar, sifted
- ○ 1½ tsp. butter, softened

# Grasshopper Brownies

Preheat oven to 350°. Generously grease a 9 x 13" baking pan; set aside. In a large mixing bowl, beat together ½ cup butter and sugar on medium speed until light and fluffy. Beat in eggs, flour, salt, chocolate syrup and vanilla until well blended. Spread batter in prepared pan and bake for 25 to 30 minutes or until brownies test almost done with a toothpick. Let cool completely.

In a small bowl, stir together 1 tablespoon crème de menthe and 1 tablespoon chocolate liqueur. Brush mixture on brownies; let stand 5 minutes.

Meanwhile, in a medium mixing bowl, beat together remaining ½ cup butter, powdered sugar, remaining 2 tablespoons crème de menthe and mint extract on medium speed until smooth and light. Spread frosting on brownie layer in pan; set aside.

In a medium saucepan over medium-high heat, bring whipping cream to a boil. Remove from heat and add chocolate chips. Let stand for 5 minutes without stirring. Stir until smooth. Stir in remaining 2 tablespoons chocolate liqueur until blended. Cool for 15 minutes. Spread over mint frosting layer. Cover and chill 1 hour or until set. Cut into bars.

**Serves 30**

## You Will Need:

- 1 C. butter, softened, divided
- 1 C. sugar
- 4 eggs, beaten
- 1 C. flour
- ½ tsp. salt
- 1 (16 oz.) can chocolate syrup
- 1 tsp. vanilla extract
- 3 T. crème de menthe, divided
- 3 T. chocolate cream liqueur, divided
- 2 C. powdered sugar
- ½ tsp. mint extract
- 6 T. heavy whipping cream
- 1 (11 to 12 oz.) pkg. semi-sweet or dark chocolate chips

# Glazed Lush-ious Lemon Cake

Preheat oven to 350°. Spray a 9 x 13" baking pan with nonstick cooking spray; set aside. In a medium bowl, sift together flour, baking powder and salt; set aside. In a large mixing bowl, combine sugar and ½ cup butter. Beat on medium speed until light and fluffy. Add eggs, one at a time, beating well after each addition. Add flour mixture and buttermilk alternately to the butter mixture until blended. Beat in ¼ cup lemon juice, ¼ cup Limoncello and ¼ cup lemon zest. Spread batter in prepared pan and bake for 25 to 30 minutes or until cake tests done with a toothpick. Cool completely. Brush top of cake with 2 tablespoons Limoncello.

In a small saucepan over low heat, combine remaining 3 tablespoons butter, ¾ cup powdered sugar and remaining 3 tablespoons lemon juice, 3 tablespoons Limoncello and 1½ teaspoons lemon zest. Stir until butter melts and mixture comes to a simmer. Whisk in additional powdered sugar, by tablespoonful, until glaze reaches desired drizzling consistency.

To assemble dessert, cut cake into small cubes. Arrange a layer of cubes in each dessert dish and sprinkle with a few blueberries. Spoon half of warm glaze over cake and berries. Add another layer of cake cubes, blueberries and remaining glaze. Just before serving, add a swirl of whipped topping.

## You Will Need:

**Serves 10**

- ○ 2 C. cake flour
- ○ 1½ tsp. baking powder
- ○ ½ tsp. salt
- ○ 1½ C. sugar
- ○ ½ C. plus 3 T. butter, softened, divided
- ○ 4 eggs
- ○ ¾ C. buttermilk
- ○ ¼ C. plus 3 T. lemon juice, divided
- ○ ¼ C. plus 5 T. Limoncello (lemon liqueur), divided
- ○ ¼ C. plus 1½ tsp. finely grated lemon zest, divided
- ○ ¾ C. plus 6 T. powdered sugar, sifted, divided
- ○ 1 pt. fresh blueberries
- ○ Spray whipped topping (such as Reddi-wip)

# Strawberry Tipsy Torte

Preheat oven to 350°. In a medium bowl, stir together flour, pecans and brown sugar. With a pastry blender or two knives, cut in butter until crumbly. Press mixture in the bottom of an ungreased 9" springform pan. Bake for 15 to 20 minutes or until lightly browned. Let cool completely.

In a medium mixing bowl, beat cream cheese on medium speed until smooth and creamy. Slowly blend in milk. Mix in rum. Add pudding mix and beat on low speed for 1 minute or until thickened. Pour over cooled crust, spreading evenly. Arrange sliced strawberries in a circular pattern on top of pudding layer as desired, starting around outer edge. Cut berries into smaller pieces as needed. Place whole berry in the middle, pointed side up. Refrigerate while preparing topping.

In a large microwave-safe measuring cup, bring ¾ cup water to a boil. Add gelatin and stir until completely dissolved, about 2 minutes. Stir in ½ cup cold water and triple sec until blended. Slowly pour gelatin mixture over strawberries. Refrigerate at least 3 hours or until set.

To serve, loosen filling from side of pan with a knife dipped in hot water. Carefully remove side of pan and slice into wedges.

**Serves 10**

## You Will Need:

- ⅔ C. flour
- 3 T. finely chopped pecans
- 2 T. brown sugar
- ⅓ C. butter, softened
- 1 (8 oz.) pkg. cream cheese, softened
- 1 C. milk
- ⅓ C. light rum
- 1 (3.4 oz.) pkg. lemon instant pudding mix
- 3 C. sliced fresh strawberries, plus 1 whole berry
- 1 (3 oz.) pkg. strawberry gelatin
- ¼ C. triple sec

# Pear Martini Crisp

Preheat oven to 350°. Spray an 8" round cake pan or 9" pie plate with non-stick cooking spray; set aside. In a medium bowl, stir together ⅓ cup vodka, lemon juice, 2 teaspoons cinnamon, nutmeg and ¼ cup brown sugar. Measure 1½ tablespoons of vodka mixture into a small bowl; set aside. To remaining vodka mixture in medium bowl, add pears and toss until fruit is completely glazed. Pour mixture into prepared pan; set aside.

In a medium microwave-safe bowl, melt ⅓ cup butter. Stir in flour, walnuts and ⅔ cup brown sugar until well combined and crumbly. Sprinkle mixture evenly over pears.

Bake for 35 to 40 minutes or until topping is golden brown and filling is bubbly. Remove from oven and let cool.

In a small saucepan over medium heat, combine remaining 3 tablespoons butter and remaining 1 cup brown sugar. Boil for about 5 minutes, stirring constantly until smooth. Remove from heat and stir in corn syrup. Cool caramel sauce for 15 minutes. Add set-aside vodka mixture and stir well.

In a chilled medium mixing bowl with chilled beaters, beat whipping cream and sugar on high speed until stiff peaks form. Stir in remaining 2 tablespoons vodka.

## To Serve

Spoon pear crisp into individual serving bowls. Top with caramel sauce and whipped cream. Sprinkle lightly with cinnamon, if desired.

**Serves 8**

## You Will Need:

- ⅓ C. plus 2 T. pear or vanilla vodka, divided
- 1 T. lemon juice
- 2 tsp. ground cinnamon, plus more for sprinkling, divided
- ¼ tsp. ground nutmeg
- 1¼ C. plus ⅔ C. brown sugar, divided
- 4½ C. fresh pears, peeled, cored, sliced
- ⅔ C. flour
- ⅔ C. coarsely chopped walnuts
- ⅓ C. plus 3 T. butter, divided
- 1½ tsp. light corn syrup
- 1 C. heavy whipping cream
- 2 T. sugar

# Toasted Piña Colada Pie

Preheat oven to 350°. Crush ¼ cup toasted coconut and set aside. Coarsely break up 2 tablespoons toasted almonds and reserve for later use. Spray a 9" pie plate (4-cup capacity) with nonstick cooking spray; set aside. In a medium bowl, stir together graham cracker crumbs, sugar, butter and crushed coconut until well mixed. Press mixture evenly in the bottom and up the sides of prepared pie plate. Bake for 10 to 12 minutes or until slightly browned. Let cool in pan for 30 minutes.

Meanwhile, in a large microwave-safe measuring cup, bring ⅔ cup water to a boil. Add gelatin and stir until completely dissolved, about 2 minutes; set aside. In a medium mixing bowl, beat cream cheese on medium speed until creamy. Gradually beat in gelatin mixture. Whisk in pineapple, coconut rum and 1 cup whipped topping until thoroughly blended. Sprinkle reserved broken almonds over graham cracker crust. Spread cream cheese filling evenly in crust. Refrigerate 3 hours or overnight.

Before serving, cut into wedges and top with dollops of remaining whipped topping. Garnish with remaining toasted coconut and almonds.

• To toast, place coconut and almonds on separate baking sheets in a 350° oven for about 10 minutes or until evenly browned, stirring occasionally.

## You Will Need:

**Serves 4**

- ½ C. sweetened flaked coconut, toasted*, divided
- ¼ C. sliced almonds, toasted*
- 1¼ C. graham cracker crumbs
- 2 T. sugar
- ⅓ C. butter, melted
- 1 (3 oz.) pkg. island pineapple gelatin
- 4 oz. cream cheese, softened
- 1 (8 oz.) can crushed pineapple
- 3 T. coconut rum
- 2 C. whipped topping, divided

# Spiked Eggnog Cream Puffs

Preheat oven to 400°. In a medium saucepan over medium-high heat, combine 1 cup water and butter. Bring mixture to a rolling boil. Reduce heat to low and stir in flour, beating vigorously until mixture forms a ball, about 1 minute. Remove from heat and let stand for 1 to 2 minutes. Beat in eggs all at once, whisking until smooth. Drop dough onto ungreased baking sheet by scant ¼ cupfuls, placing puffs about 3" apart. Bake for 35 to 40 minutes or until puffed and golden brown. Cool completely on baking sheets.

Meanwhile, in a medium mixing bowl, beat together pudding mix, milk, rum, nutmeg and ginger on medium speed until well blended, about 1 minute. Add whipping cream and beat on high speed until soft peaks form, about 2 minutes. Cover and chill at least 30 minutes or until needed.

To assemble, cut off tops of cooled puffs and pull out any filaments of soft dough. Spoon or pipe chilled filling into the bottom half of each puff and replace top. Serve immediately or cover and refrigerate no longer than 3 hours. Just before serving, sprinkle with powdered sugar.

## You Will Need:

**Serves 12**

- ½ C. butter
- 1 C. flour
- 4 eggs, lightly beaten
- 1 (3.4 oz.) pkg. vanilla instant pudding mix
- ½ C. milk
- ⅓ C. light rum (or less to taste)
- 1 tsp. ground nutmeg
- ¼ tsp. ground ginger
- 1¼ C. heavy whipping cream
- Powdered sugar

# Loaded Sandwich Cookies

Preheat oven to 350°. In a large bowl, combine cake mix, butter and egg. Mix well with a spoon. Firmly shape dough into 1¼" balls. (You'll need two balls for each sandwich cookie.) Place balls 2" apart on ungreased baking sheets. Bake for 10 to 13 minutes or until set and cracked on top. Cool cookies on baking sheet for 1 minute before removing to a wire rack to cool completely.

Prepare one of the fillings below. Pipe or spread chilled filling on the flat side of half the cookies; top with remaining cookies. Refrigerate until serving.

### Peanut Butter

In a medium bowl, beat together 4 ounces softened cream cheese, 6 tablespoons creamy peanut butter and ½ teaspoon vanilla on medium speed until creamy. Beat in 2 cups powdered sugar. Stir in 3 tablespoons Frangelico until blended. Beat in ½ cup additional powdered sugar. Chill for 30 minutes.

### Raspberry

In a medium bowl, beat together 4 ounces softened cream cheese, 6 tablespoons softened butter and ½ teaspoon vanilla on medium speed until creamy. Beat in 2 cups powdered sugar. Stir in 3 tablespoons raspberry schnapps and 2 to 3 tablespoons seedless raspberry preserves until blended. Beat in ½ cup additional powdered sugar. Tint with red food coloring as desired. Chill for 30 minutes.

### Peppermint

In a medium bowl, beat together 4 ounces softened cream cheese, 6 tablespoons softened butter and ½ teaspoon vanilla on medium speed until creamy. Beat in 2 cups powdered sugar. Stir in 3 tablespoons peppermint schnapps and ¼ teaspoon peppermint extract until blended. Beat in ½ cup additional powdered sugar. Chill for 30 minutes.

## You Will Need:

**Serves 12**

- ○ 1 (18.25 oz.) pkg. dark chocolate cake mix (pudding type)
- ○ ½ C. butter, melted
- ○ 1 egg, slightly beaten
- ○ Creamy Filling (choose Peanut Butter, Raspberry or Peppermint)

# Boozy Brownie Swirls

Preheat oven to 350°. Spray nine 6-ounce ramekins or a muffin pan with nonstick cooking spray; set aside. In a large mixing bowl, combine brownie mix with oil and eggs as directed on package, stirring in beer in place of water. Divide batter evenly among prepared ramekins; set aside.

In a medium mixing bowl, beat together cream cheese and sugar on medium speed until well combined and creamy. Beat in egg until thoroughly mixed. Stir in Irish cream. Spoon mixture evenly over brownie batter in ramekins. Using a fork or knife, gently swirl mixtures.

Set ramekins on a baking sheet and bake for 35 to 40 minutes or until the middle is just set and small cracks begin to form. Cool completely.

## You Will Need:

Serves 9

- 1 (18 to 20 oz.) pkg. brownie mix
- Vegetable oil and eggs as directed on brownie mix package
- ¼ C. stout beer
- 1 (8 oz.) pkg. cream cheese, softened
- ⅓ C. sugar
- 1 egg
- 2 T. Irish cream

# Rum-Spiked Cherry Cobbler

Preheat oven to 375°. Lightly spray four 8-ounce ramekins with cooking spray; set aside. In a large skillet over medium heat, melt ¼ cup butter. Add 3 tablespoons brown sugar, stirring to combine. Add cherries and ¼ cup rum. Cook, stirring frequently, about 5 minutes. Using a slotted spoon, transfer cherries to a large bowl; reserve juice in skillet.

To cherries in bowl, add 2 tablespoons brown sugar, 1 tablespoon cornstarch and cinnamon. Mix well to evenly coat cherries; set aside.

In a medium bowl, stir together flour, sugar, remaining 2 tablespoons brown sugar, baking powder and salt. Cut remaining 6 tablespoons butter into small pieces. Add to flour mixture and combine with a pastry blender or two knives until mixture resembles coarse crumbs. Add ¼ cup whipping cream and mix just until dough comes together in a ball.

Place prepared ramekins on a baking sheet. Divide cherries evenly between ramekins and bake for about 5 minutes or just until heated through. Remove from oven and drop pieces of dough over warm cherries. Brush dough with a little whipping cream and sprinkle with coarse sugar. Return to oven and bake for 20 to 25 minutes or until topping is golden brown and filling is bubbly. Remove from oven.

In a small bowl, stir together remaining 2 teaspoons cornstarch and 1 tablespoon cold water, stirring until cornstarch is dissolved and mixture is smooth. Add to reserved juice in skillet. Stir in almond extract. Cook and stir over medium-low heat until slightly thickened. Remove from heat and cool slightly. Stir in remaining 2 tablespoons rum and serve with cobbler.

## You Will Need:

**Serves 4**

- ¼ C. plus 6 T. butter, divided
- 7 T. brown sugar, divided
- 2 (12 oz.) bags frozen dark sweet cherries
- ¼ C. plus 2 T. light rum, divided
- 1 T. plus 2 tsp. cornstarch, divided
- ¼ tsp. ground cinnamon
- 1⅓ C. flour
- 2 T. sugar
- 1 tsp. baking powder
- ⅛ tsp. salt
- ¼ C. heavy whipping cream, plus more for brushing
- ¼ C. coarse sugar
- ¼ tsp. almond extract

# Punchy Crunchy Pecan Pie

Preheat oven to 350°. Lightly spray a 10" pie plate with nonstick cooking spray; set aside. In a medium bowl, combine flour, shortening and ½ teaspoon salt, using a pastry blender or two knives to blend together until fine crumbs form. Stir in milk, a little at a time, until dough begins to hold together, but isn't sticky. On a floured surface, roll dough into a 13" circle, about ¼" thick. Carefully transfer dough to prepared pie plate**, pressing gently, without stretching, in the bottom and up the sides of plate. Trim off excess dough and flute edges. Place in freezer while making filling.

In a medium bowl, whisk eggs until frothy. Add ground pecans, ½ cup bourbon, 2 cups sugar, butter and remaining ¼ teaspoon salt, mixing to combine thoroughly. Stir in chopped pecans and 1 cup whole pecans.

Remove pie crust from freezer and pour filling mixture into crust. Place pie on a baking sheet. Bake for 45 to 65 minutes or until crust is golden brown and center of filling is slightly puffed. Filling may be slightly soft in the center. Remove pie from baking sheet and cool completely. Refrigerate several hours before cutting into wedges.

In a small bowl, beat whipping cream and remaining 1 teaspoon sugar until soft peaks form. Add remaining 1 tablespoon bourbon and beat until stiff peaks form. Top pie with dollops of whipped cream and garnish with remaining whole pecans. Serve promptly.

**Serves 8**

## You Will Need:

- ○ 1½ C. flour
- ○ ½ C. vegetable shortening
- ○ ¾ tsp. salt, divided
- ○ 3 to 3½ T. milk
- ○ 6 eggs
- ○ 1 C. ground pecans
- ○ ½ C. plus 1 T. bourbon, divided
- ○ 2 C. plus 1 tsp. sugar, divided
- ○ ¼ C. melted butter
- ○ 1 C. chopped pecans, toasted*
- ○ 1 C. plus 8 whole pecans, toasted*, divided
- ○ 1 C. heavy whipping cream

\* To toast, place pecans on a baking sheet in a 350° oven for about 10 minutes or until evenly browned, stirring occasionally.

\*\* After rolling dough, carefully fold in half and remove from the work surface using a large metal spatula. Place in the center of prepared pan and unfold.

# Boozed-Up Banana Trifle

In a small bowl, mix 2 tablespoons rum and 2 tablespoons bourbon. Arrange 50 to 60 vanilla wafers on a rimmed baking sheet and brush lightly with rum mixture; set aside.

In a large saucepan over medium-low heat, combine milk with pudding mixes, whisking to blend well. Cook, stirring constantly, until mixture thickens and comes to a full boil. Remove from heat. Place plastic wrap on surface of pudding; let cool for 10 minutes before whisking in remaining ½ cup rum. Refrigerate until assembly.

Peel and slice bananas. To assemble trifle, arrange about ⅓ of the prepared wafers in the bottom and up the sides of a deep 2½-quart glass bowl. Place about ⅓ of the sliced bananas over wafers and against side of

bowl. Spread ⅓ of the pudding mixture over bananas. Sprinkle ⅓ of the toffee bits generously around edge of bowl and over top of pudding. Repeat with two more layers of wafers, bananas, pudding and toffee bits. Refrigerate at least 1 hour.

In a chilled bowl with chilled beaters, beat whipping cream with sugar until soft peaks form. Stir in remaining 1 tablespoon bourbon. Before serving, place dollops of whipped cream on trifle and garnish with plain wafers as desired.

## You Will Need:

Serves
12

- ○  2 T. plus ½ C. light rum, divided
- ○  3 T. bourbon, divided
- ○  1 (12 oz. box) vanilla wafers (there will be extras)
- ○  7 C. milk
- ○  4 (3 oz.) pkgs. vanilla cook-and-serve pudding mix
- ○  8 bananas
- ○  1½ C. milk chocolate toffee bits
- ○  1 C. heavy whipping cream
- ○  1 T. sugar

# Chocolate Raspberry Cups

Line 15 mini muffin cups with paper liners; set aside. In a microwave-safe bowl, melt chocolate chips, stirring until smooth. Add butter and shortening; stir until melted and smooth. Spoon 1 tablespoon of melted mixture into a paper liner. With a small paintbrush, coat the inside of liner with a layer of chocolate, from bottom toward top edge. Repeat to make additional cups. Chill until set. Brush on a second layer of chocolate and refrigerate until set. Before using, gently peel off paper liners and refrigerate chocolate cups until ready to use.

In a small chilled mixing bowl with chilled beaters, beat whipping cream on high speed until stiff peaks form. Stir in chocolate syrup and raspberry schnapps until well combined. Spoon mixture into chocolate cups and freeze for several hours. Serve immediately after removing from freezer. These treats do not freeze solid.

## You Will Need:

**Serves 15**

- ○ 1½ C. semi-sweet chocolate chips
- ○ 3 T. butter
- ○ 3 to 4 tsp. vegetable shortening
- ○ 1 C. heavy whipping cream
- ○ ¾ C. chocolate syrup
- ○ 2 T. raspberry schnapps

# Grown-Up S'Mores

Preheat oven to 375°. Spray four 8-ounce ramekins with nonstick cooking spray; set aside. In a shallow bowl, stir together coffee and Frangelico. Break graham crackers into pieces to fit ramekins. Dip both sides of a few graham cracker pieces into coffee mixture and arrange in a single layer in the bottom of each ramekin. Top each with ¼ of a candy bar.

Using kitchen shears dipped in water, cut each marshmallow into four crosswise slices and place four or five slices on each candy bar piece. Repeat layers two times until ramekins are full. Reserve remaining coffee mixture.

Set ramekins on a baking sheet. Bake for 12 to 15 minutes or until chocolate is soft and top marshmallow pieces are toasty brown. Remove from oven and drizzle about 1 tablespoon coffee mixture over each ramekin. Serve warm.

* Amaretto also tastes delicious.

## You Will Need:

Serves 4

- ½ C. brewed coffee, cooled
- ¼ C. Frangelico (hazelnut liqueur)*
- 12 graham cracker squares
- 16 regular-sized marshmallows
- 3 (1.55 oz.) milk chocolate candy bars

# Black Forest Brownies

Preheat oven to 350°. Lightly spray two 8" round baking pans with nonstick cooking spray. Line bottom of pans with parchment paper and spray again; set aside. Combine brownie mix with water, oil and egg as directed on package. Divide batter between prepared pans and bake as directed for a 9x13" pan. Cool completely.

In a small bowl, stir together pie filling, 1 tablespoon cherry brandy and ½ teaspoon almond extract; set aside.

In a medium chilled mixing bowl with chilled beaters, beat whipping cream until frothy. Gradually beat in powdered sugar on high speed until stiff peaks form. Stir in remaining ½ teaspoon almond extract and 1 tablespoon cherry brandy.

Remove brownies from pan and peel off parchment paper. Trim edge of one brownie as needed to fit the bottom of an 8" round dessert dish (2½ to 3 quarts)*, using removed parchment paper as a guide. Place brownie in dish. Brush top of brownie with 1 tablespoon cherry brandy. Reserve about 12 whole cherries from pie filling; spoon remaining pie filling over brownie. Spread half of whipped cream over cherry layer. Trim remaining brownie as needed to fit next layer in dessert dish; set brownie on top of whipped cream layer. Brush top of brownie with remaining 1 tablespoon cherry brandy. Top with remaining whipped cream. Cut trimmed brownies into small cubes. Garnish dessert with reserved cherries and brownie cubes as desired.

* Or, simply cut each brownie into 1" pieces, layer pieces in the dish and drizzle with cherry brandy while assembling layers as directed.

## You Will Need:

**Serves 16**

- O   1 (18.3 oz.) pkg. fudge brownie mix
- O   Water, vegetable oil and egg as directed on brownie mix package
- O   1 (21 oz.) can cherry pie filling
- O   ¼ C. cherry brandy, divided
- O   1 tsp. almond extract, divided
- O   2 C. heavy whipping cream
- O   ½ C. powdered sugar

# Jammin' Vanilla Cheesecake

Preheat oven to 350°. Spray an 8" square baking pan with nonstick cooking spray; set aside. In a medium bowl, combine shortening and brown sugar; mix with a spoon until creamy and well blended. Add flour, oats and salt, mixing thoroughly until crumbly. Press dough in prepared pan. Bake for 15 to 17 minutes or until golden brown. Let cool completely.

In a small bowl, whisk together preserves and 2 teaspoons vanilla vodka. Spread over cooled crust and set aside.

In a small saucepan, combine 8 teaspoons vanilla vodka and 4 teaspoons vanilla. Sprinkle gelatin over mixture and let stand for 10 minutes. Place saucepan over low heat and stir just until dissolved. Cool to barely lukewarm. Meanwhile, in a large mixing bowl, combine cream cheese, $2/3$ cup sugar and 1½ teaspoons vanilla. Beat at medium speed until smooth and creamy. Beat in whipping cream. Add gelatin mixture and beat until

blended. Spread cream cheese mixture over preserves. Cover and refrigerate 5 hours or overnight.

In a small bowl, combine raspberries with remaining 5 teaspoons vanilla vodka, 2 teaspoons vanilla and ¼ cup sugar. Let stand 15 minutes. To serve, cut dessert into squares and top with raspberry mixture.

## You Will Need:

Serves
9

- ⅓ C. vegetable shortening
- 3 T. brown sugar
- ⅔ C. flour
- ½ C. quick-cooking oats
- ⅛ tsp. salt
- ½ C. seedless raspberry preserves
- 5 T. vanilla vodka, divided
- 7½ tsp. vanilla extract, divided
- ½ tsp. unflavored gelatin
- 2 (8 oz.) pkgs. cream cheese, softened
- ⅔ C. plus ¼ C. sugar, divided
- 6 T. heavy whipping cream
- 2 C. frozen raspberries, thawed

# Poked Cake Shots

Preheat oven to 350°. Spray bottom of a 12 x 18" jelly roll pan with nonstick cooking spray; set aside. In a large mixing bowl, combine cake mix with water, oil and egg whites as directed on package. Spread batter in prepared pan and bake for 12 to 15 minutes or until cake tests done with a toothpick. Cool cake in pan for 15 minutes. With a large fork, poke cake at ½" intervals without piercing all the way through.

Place gelatin in a medium bowl and add 3 cups boiling water, stirring for 2 minutes or until completely dissolved. Stir in ¾ cup cold water, raspberry schnapps and almond liqueur until blended. Pour 1 to 1½ cups of gelatin mixture over cake, allowing it to soak into holes. Refrigerate 3 hours.

Pour remaining gelatin mixture into small dessert dishes or shot glasses (2- to 4-ounce capacity), filling each one halfway. Refrigerate until set.

To assemble, use a round cookie cutter that matches the size of dessert dishes or shot glasses being used**. Spray cutter lightly with nonstick cooking spray; cut one round of chilled cake for each dessert. Carefully set cake round over gelatin layer in each dish or glass, pressing gently until cake rests on gelatin. Refrigerate until serving time. Top with whipped topping and colored sprinkles, if desired.

* Number of servings depends on size of containers used.
** You may also cut out cake rounds using a drinking glass lightly sprayed with nonstick cooking spray.

**Serves 24\***

## You Will Need:

- ○ 1 (18.25 oz.) pkg. white cake mix
- ○ Water, vegetable oil and egg whites as directed on cake mix package
- ○ 3 (3 oz.) pkgs. raspberry gelatin
- ○ ½ C. plus 1 T. raspberry schnapps
- ○ 3 T. crème de almond liqueur
- ○ Whipped topping
- ○ Colored sprinkles, optional

## Great flavor combos:

Lime gelatin + vanilla vodka or lime vodka

Berry Blue gelatin + blue curaçao

Peach gelatin + peach schnapps

Tropical Fusion gelatin + light rum

Cherry gelatin + cherry brandy

(Use 3 packages of gelatin with ¾ cup alcohol and water as directed above.)

# Schnapp-y Chocolate Cake Balls

Preheat oven to 350°. Spray a 9 x 13" baking pan with nonstick cooking spray; set aside. In a large mixing bowl, combine cake mix with water, oil and eggs as directed on package. Spread batter in prepared pan and bake according to package instructions for pan size. Let cool completely.

Cut cake into pieces and use hands to crumble the cake into a large bowl. Add crushed Oreos and mix well with a spoon. Stir in peppermint schnapps, a little at a time, until mixture holds together like thick moist dough. Cover bowl and refrigerate at least 2 hours or overnight.

Line a baking sheet with waxed paper. Form dough into small firm balls, 1" to 1½" in diameter. Place on prepared baking sheet and freeze at least 3 hours or until very firm.

In a large microwave-safe measuring cup, melt chocolate chips, stirring until smooth. Reserve ¼ cup chopped candy. Stir remaining candy into chocolate until melted. With a toothpick, dip one frozen cake ball into melted chocolate to coat, gently tapping toothpick on the side of measuring cup to let excess chocolate drip back into cup. Place on waxed paper, remove toothpick and fill in hole with a drop of melted chocolate. Immediately sprinkle top with reserved chopped candy before chocolate sets. Work in small batches, leaving remaining cake balls in the freezer until dipping. Serve cold or at room temperature.

## You Will Need:

Serves 50

- 1 (18.25 oz.) pkg. chocolate cake mix
- Water, vegetable oil and eggs as directed on cake mix package
- 15 mint Oreo cookies, crushed (about 2 C.)
- ¾ to 1 C. peppermint schnapps
- 2 (12 oz.) pkgs. milk chocolate chips
- 1 (4.67 oz.) pkg. Andes crème de menthe candies (about 28), chopped, divided

# Cheeky Chocolate Fondue

In a large glass measuring cup, combine whipping cream and orange zest. Microwave until hot, about 60 seconds. Add chocolate chips and let stand for 1 to 2 minutes to soften; stir to mix. Add coffee and corn syrup; stir until smooth. Whisk in Grand Marnier. Transfer mixture to a fondue pot or a glass bowl set over hot water and serve warm with skewers of strawberries, apples, pineapple and apricots for dipping.

## You Will Need:

- 6 T. heavy whipping cream
- 1 tsp. grated orange zest
- 1 C. plus 2 T. semi-sweet chocolate chips
- ½ tsp. instant coffee granules dissolved in ½ tsp. hot water
- 2 T. light corn syrup
- 3 T. Grand Marnier liqueur
- **Dippers:** fresh strawberries, green and red apple wedges*, dried pineapple chunks, dried apricots

* Dip sliced apples in lemon juice to prevent browning; drain well.

**Serves 8**

# Punchy Peach Fondue

In a large glass measuring cup, microwave whipping cream until very hot, 1½ to 2 minutes. Add white chips and let stand for 1 to 2 minutes to soften. Whisk until smooth. Stir in peach puree. Whisk in rum. Transfer mixture to a fondue pot or a glass bowl set over hot water and serve warm with skewers of angel food cake cubes, shortbread or meringue cookies, marshmallows, pretzels or ladyfingers. Sauce may also be served cold.

## You Will Need:

- ¾ C. heavy whipping cream
- 1 (12 oz.) pkg. white baking chips
- 2 (15 oz.) cans peaches, drained, pureed
- ¼ C. light rum, white chocolate liqueur or peach schnapps
- **Dippers:** angel food cake cubes, shortbread cookies, meringue cookies, marshmallows, pretzels, ladyfingers

**Serves 20**

# Raspberry & Chocolate Shot

Line 8 to 10 jumbo muffin cups with paper liners and set aside. In a large mixing bowl, combine cake mix, water, oil and eggs; mix as directed on package. Stir in raspberry flavoring. Spoon batter into prepared pans, filling cups 2/3 to ¾ full. Bake for 18 to 20 minutes or until cupcakes test done with a toothpick.

Drain raspberries, reserving 3 tablespoons juice. Press berries through a sieve to remove seeds and obtain about ¼ cup raspberry puree; discard seeds and set aside puree. Sprinkle gelatin over 1 tablespoon reserved raspberry juice; let stand 1 minute to soften. Boil remaining 2 tablespoons reserved juice and pour over gelatin; stir until gelatin is completely dissolved. In a chilled mixing bowl with chilled beaters, beat whipping cream, powdered sugar and vanilla until soft peaks form. Pour gelatin mixture into whipped cream mixture and beat until almost stiff. Carefully fold in raspberry puree and red food coloring, if desired. Refrigerate for 30 minutes.

With a small cookie cutter or knife, cut a round hole in the top and toward one side of each cupcake, as wide and nearly as deep as the chocolate shot glass. Frost tops of cupcakes with raspberry mixture. Insert a white chocolate shot glass in each hole and fill with 2 teaspoons raspberry schnapps. To imbibe, hold the cupcake like a drink, bring it to your mouth, tip your head back and guzzle the schnapps. Eat the cupcake and shot glass as the chaser.

## White Chocolate Shot Glasses

- 1 C. white chocolate baking chips (or other flavors/colors)
- 1 tsp. vegetable shortening (white)

In a microwave-safe bowl, combine baking chips and shortening. Microwave until melted and smooth, stirring every 30 seconds. Spoon 1 teaspoon of melted mixture into a mini muffin paper liner. With a small paintbrush, coat the inside of liner with a layer of chocolate, from bottom toward top edge. Repeat to make additional cups. Chill for 10 minutes or until set. Brush on a second layer and let dry. Before using, gently peel off paper liners. Set cups into holes in cupcakes and fill with booze.

### You Will Need:

**Serves 10**

- 1 (18.25) oz. pkg. devil's food cake mix (pudding type)
- Water, vegetable oil and eggs as directed on cake mix package
- 1 to 2 tsp. raspberry flavoring
- 1 (10 oz.) pkg. frozen red raspberries, thawed
- 1 tsp. unflavored gelatin
- 1 C. heavy whipping cream
- ¼ C. powdered sugar
- ½ tsp. vanilla extract
- Red food coloring, optional
- 8 to 10 white chocolate shot glasses (see above)
- ½ C. raspberry schnapps

4 oz. alcohol

# More Shots & Shooters

### 4th of July

**Shot glasses**: Red shot glasses made from 30 red vanilla-flavored candy wafers

**Cupcakes**: White cupcakes. Poke holes and brush tops with vodka. Fill holes with grenadine.

**Frosting**: Ready-to-use fluffy white frosting and red/white/blue sprinkles

**Shot of booze**: blue curaçao

### Santa Baby

**Shot glasses**: Red shot glasses made from 30 red vanilla-flavored candy wafers

**Cupcakes**: White cupcakes. Poke holes and fill with grenadine or green crème de menthe.

**Frosting**: Fluffy white or cream cheese frosting, stirring in mint flavoring to taste and a small amount of crème de menthe, if desired

**Shot of booze**: peppermint schnapps or green crème de menthe

### Lemon Drop

**Shot glasses**: Yellow shot glasses made with 30 yellow vanilla-flavored candy wafers

**Cupcakes**: Lemon cupcakes. Inject each cupcake with about 5 ml. vodka.

**Topping**: Dip cupcake tops in lemon juice and then in coarse white sparkling sugar to coat generously.

**Shot of booze**: vodka

## Polar Bear

**Shot glasses:** White chocolate shot glasses as directed

**Cupcakes:** Chocolate cupcakes with 1 to 2 teaspoons peppermint flavoring stirred into batter. If desired, inject cupcakes with peppermint schnapps and/or white crème de cacao.

**Frosting:** Fluffy white frosting

**Shooter of booze:** 1 teaspoon each peppermint schnapps and dark crème de cacao

## Chocolate Heaven

**Shot glasses:** Chocolate shot glasses made with 30 chocolate candy wafers

**Cupcakes:** Chocolate cupcakes. In a small bowl, stir together 2 teaspoons each Irish cream, chocolate cream liqueur and Kahlúa; poke cupcakes and brush booze mixture over the top.

**Frosting:** Caramel frosting

**Shooter of booze:** ½ teaspoon each Irish cream, chocolate cream liqueur and Kahlúa

## Tool Kit

**Shot glasses:** White chocolate shot glasses as directed

**Cupcakes:** White cupcakes. In a small bowl, stir together 1½ teaspoons each Irish cream, crème de cacao, amaretto and Kahlúa. Poke cupcakes and brush booze mixture over the top.

**Frosting:** Chocolate frosting

**Shooter of booze:** ½ teaspoon each Irish cream, crème de cacao, amaretto and Kahlúa

# Shot-sicles & Other Frozen Treats

## Recipes in this chapter are based on the following serving sizes:

Popsicles: 3-ounce molds

Granita-type mixtures: 4 ounces

Smoothies and other iced drinks:
8 ounces

## Tipsy Tips to Remember

○ A smoothie maker may be used in place of a blender for blended mixtures.

○ When pouring mixture into molds for popsicles, leave about ¼" headspace (some molds indicate fill lines).

○ When a recipe calls for a carbonated beverage, leave extra headspace for expansion; do not seal, but cover lightly with foil or plastic wrap instead.

○ When freezing creamy mixtures, choose molds without sharp corners for best results.

○ To fill molds easily, combine mixtures in spouted bowls or measuring cups.

○ In place of standard popsicle molds, you can use small paper cups or other small containers and insert sticks when mixture is partially set. Peel off paper cups or remove from containers to serve.

○ Try a variety of sticks with your popsicle molds such as hors d'oeuvre picks, swizzle sticks and wooden popsicle sticks or skewers.

○ If necessary, hold sticks upright in molds by covering with heavy-duty aluminum foil and inserting sticks in the center. Support with tape as needed.

○ To remove popsicles from molds, hold mold between hands or run under warm water for a few seconds.

○ To refreeze popsicles after removing from molds, set them on a platter and return to freezer before serving.

○ To freeze granita-type mixtures, choose a pan (such as a 9" square pan) that keeps the level of the mixture shallow, allowing it to freeze quickly and evenly.

Bombed Pops, page 124.

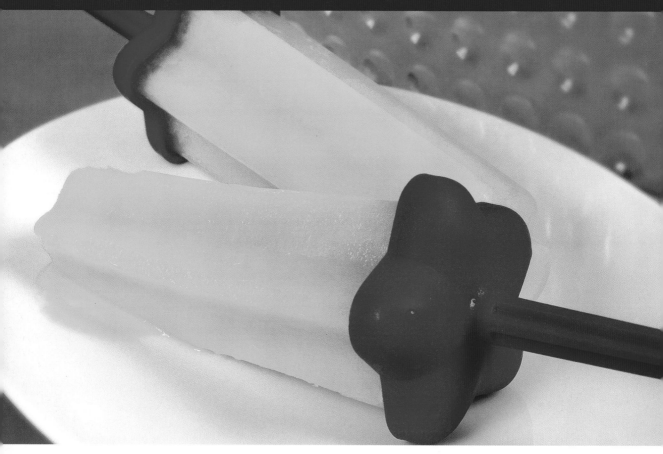

# Mango Pops

In a blender, combine mango, 2 tablespoons water, rum, sugar and lime juice. Blend until smooth. Press mixture through a strainer; discard solids. Pour liquid into molds. Freeze at least 24 hours.

## You Will Need:

- 3 C. peeled and chopped ripe mango
- 6 T. light rum
- ½ C. sugar
- 1½ T. lime juice

**Serves 6**

# Piña Colada Pops

In a blender, combine pudding mix, milk, lime juice and rum; blend until smooth. Add pineapple with juice and pulse to incorporate. Pour into molds and freeze overnight or until solid.

## You Will Need:

○ 1 (3.4 oz.) pkg. coconut cream instant pudding mix
○ 1½ C. milk
○ 1 T. lime juice
○ ¼ C. light rum
○ 1 (8 oz.) can crushed pineapple

**Serves 10**

# Mudsicle Squares

In a small bowl, stir together cookie crumbs, ½ cup pecans, 1 tablespoon Kahlúa and butter. Press in the bottom of a 9 x 13" baking pan; set aside.

In a large mixing bowl, beat cream cheese on medium speed until light and fluffy. Blend in 1½ tablespoons Kahlúa, sweetened condensed milk and ½ cup chocolate syrup. Set aside ½ cup whipped topping. Blend remaining whipped topping into chocolate mixture; spread over crust. Cover and freeze overnight before cutting into squares.

In a small bowl, stir together milk, remaining ¼ cup chocolate syrup, remaining 2 tablespoons Kahlúa and reserved ½ cup whipped topping. Drizzle over dessert squares before serving.

## You Will Need:

**Serves 24**

- 1½ C. cream-filled chocolate cookie crumbs
- ¾ C. ground pecans, divided
- 4½ T. Kahlúa (coffee liqueur), divided
- ¼ C. melted butter
- 2 (8 oz.) pkgs. cream cheese, softened
- 1 (14 oz.) can sweetened condensed milk
- ¾ C. chocolate syrup, divided
- 1 (8 oz.) container whipped topping, divided
- ¼ C. milk

# Mimosa Ice

For Orange Mimosa, in a large measuring cup, mix orange juice, triple sec and Champagne until blended.

For Poinsettia Mimosa, in another measuring cup, mix cranberry juice and Champagne until blended.

Pour each mixture into separate shallow pans and freeze until slushy. Stir and refreeze until solid. Scrape surface with a fork and spoon layers of each mixture into chilled serving dishes.

**Serves 12**

## You Will Need:

### Orange Mimosa
- ○ 1⅔ C. orange juice
- ○ 2 T. triple sec
- ○ ⅓ C. Champagne or sparkling white wine*

### Poinsettia Mimosa
- ○ 2 C. cranberry juice
- ○ ⅓ C. Champagne or sparkling white wine*

\* Try using Moscato or Prosecco.

## Variations

To make layered popsicles, fill molds halfway with Orange Mimosa mixture, tilting the molds and taping to hold in place, if desired. Freeze several hours or until solid. Set molds upright, add sticks and fill with Poinsettia Mimosa mixture. Freeze until solid.

To make a Lilosa, use pink grapefruit juice in place of the orange juice.

# Daiquiri Pops

Prepare Simple Syrup as directed below*; let cool. For watermelon layer, place watermelon cubes in a blender and puree until smooth. Measure 1½ cups puree and add simple syrup. Strain mixture into a measuring cup and discard solids. Stir in rum.

Pour into molds filling them ⅓ full. Do not insert sticks. Freeze 4 hours or until solid.

For lime layer, combine lime juice, simple syrup, soda and ice cubes in blender and blend until smooth. Remove any remaining chunks of ice. Stir in rum. Pour mixture into molds over frozen watermelon layer, filling to ⅔ full. Freeze 2 hours or until partially set. Insert sticks, pressing the ends just into watermelon layer; freeze until solid, at least 4 hours.

For orange layer, in blender, combine mandarin oranges, lime juice, simple syrup and soda. Puree until smooth. Strain mixture into a measuring cup and discard solids. Stir in rum. Pour into molds over frozen lime layer. Freeze 8 hours or overnight.

## You Will Need:

**Serves 9**

### Watermelon Layer
- ○ 3 C. seedless watermelon cubes
- ○ 1 to 2 T. simple syrup*
- ○ 2 T. light rum

### Lime Layer
- ○ 3 T. lime juice
- ○ 3 T. simple syrup*
- ○ 1¼ C. lemon-lime soda
- ○ ¾ C. ice cubes
- ○ 2 T. light rum

### Orange Layer
- ○ 1 (15 oz.) can mandarin oranges, drained
- ○ 1 T. lime juice
- ○ 2 T. simple syrup*
- ○ 3 T. lemon-lime soda
- ○ 2 T. light rum

\* Simple Syrup: In a small saucepan over high heat, bring ½ cup water to a boil. Add ½ cup sugar and whisk until dissolved. Mixture should be clear. Cool to room temperature before using.

**Note**: For this recipe, avoid molds with stick/lid combination as sticks will be inserted partway through the freezing process.

# Root Beer Pops

Stir together root beer schnapps, root beer and softened ice cream. Pour into molds leaving extra headspace and freeze overnight or until solid. If using hollow molds*, use a melon baller to scoop additional ice cream into hollow area. Serve immediately.

* We used Prepara brand volcano ice pop molds.

## You Will Need:

- ○ 3 T. root beer schnapps
- ○ 1 C. root beer
- ○ 3 T. vanilla ice cream, softened
- ○ Additional vanilla ice cream, optional

Serves
4

# Cosmo-Sicles

In a large measuring cup, mix cranberry juice, triple sec, vodka and lime juice. Place one cranberry in each mold, if desired. Pour mixture into molds and freeze overnight or until solid.

**Serves 6**

## You Will Need:

- ○ 3 C. cranberry juice
- ○ 1 T. triple sec
- ○ 2 T. vodka
- ○ 2 T. lime juice
- ○ 6 fresh cranberries, optional

# B-52 Ice Cream Bomber

Preheat oven to 425°. Lightly grease a 9" springform pan with nonstick cooking spray; set aside. In a medium bowl, stir together cracker crumbs and butter until evenly mixed. Firmly press mixture over the bottom and about 1" up the sides of prepared pan. Bake for 5 to 7 minutes or until firm. Cool at room temperature for 20 minutes, then place in freezer for 10 minutes.

Meanwhile, in a large bowl, soften chocolate ice cream. Stir in Irish cream to blend. (Mixture should resemble a very thick milkshake.) Spread ice cream mixture over cooled crust. Cover and freeze for 1 hour or until firm on top. When chocolate ice cream is firm, soften 3 cups vanilla ice cream in a large bowl. In a small bowl, combine coffee granules with 1 teaspoon warm water; stir to dissolve. Stir coffee mixture into ice cream to blend well. Spread coffee ice cream over chocolate ice cream in pan. Cover and return to freezer for 1 hour or until firm on top. When coffee ice cream is firm, soften remaining 3 cups vanilla ice cream. Stir in orange juice concentrate and triple sec until blended. Spread orange ice cream evenly over coffee ice cream layer. Cover with foil and freeze for at least 4 hours or until firm.

Just before serving, wrap a warm wet towel around the side of pan for a few seconds to loosen cake from pan. Unhinge and remove side of pan. Slice into wedges and garnish with chocolate curls or orange slices.

## You Will Need:

**Serves 12**

- ○ 2 C. finely crushed chocolate graham crackers (about 11 rectangles)
- ○ 5 T. butter, melted
- ○ 3 C. chocolate ice cream
- ○ 2 T. Irish cream
- ○ 6 C. vanilla ice cream, divided
- ○ 1 T. instant coffee granules
- ○ 2½ T. frozen orange juice concentrate, thawed
- ○ 1½ to 2 T. triple sec
- ○ Chocolate curls or orange slices

2 oz. alcohol

# Just Peachy Bellini Pops

In a medium saucepan over high heat, stir together peaches, sugar and lemon juice. Bring to a boil. Reduce heat to medium and simmer until peaches have broken down and mixture is thick and syrupy, 10 to 15 minutes, stirring frequently. Let cool to room temperature. Transfer mixture to a blender and process until smooth. Add wine and blend briefly. Refrigerate until chilled.

Pour mixture into molds and freeze at least 6 hours or overnight. Serve promptly.

* Try using Prosecco.

### You Will Need:

Serves
10

○  4 fresh ripe peaches, peeled, pitted and chopped
○  ¾ C. sugar
○  2¼ tsp. lemon juice
○  1½ C. sparkling white wine*

# Choco~Sicles

In a large saucepan over medium heat, mix sugar, chocolate, cocoa powder, salt and 2 cups water. Bring to a boil, whisking constantly. Remove from heat; cool 30 minutes. Stir in bourbon and pour into molds. Freeze overnight.

## You Will Need:

**Serves 8**

- ½ C. sugar
- 3½ oz. bittersweet baking chocolate, chopped
- 2 T. unsweetened cocoa powder
- ⅛ tsp. salt
- 2 T. bourbon

# 'Root Beer' Slush

In a medium bowl, mix vodka, Galliano, half & half, cola and whipping cream. Freeze overnight. In a blender, process mixture until slushy. Pour into glasses and serve immediately.

**Serves 3**

## You Will Need:

- ¼ C. vodka
- ¼ C. Galliano
- ¼ C. half & half
- 2 C. cola
- 6 T. heavy whipping cream

# Cherry Vodka Granita

In a medium saucepan over medium heat, bring cherries and 1½ cups water to a boil, mashing occasionally to crush cherries. Reduce heat to low, cover loosely and simmer for 30 minutes or until cherries are soft and juice has reduced by a third.

Meanwhile, in a small saucepan over medium heat, mix sugar and 1½ cups water. Reduce heat and simmer for 30 minutes or until reduced by a third; cool.

Strain cherry mixture into a bowl, discarding solids. Add sugar mixture to cherry juice and stir in lemon juice; pour into a shallow pan. Freeze several hours, scraping mixture occasionally with a fork. Stir in vodka and cherry flavoring; refreeze until solid. Scrape with a fork and scoop into bowls. Serve immediately.

## You Will Need:

- ○ 1 (12 oz.) pkg. frozen sweet cherries
- ○ ¾ C. sugar
- ○ 1 T. lemon juice
- ○ 1 T. vodka
- ○ ¼ tsp. cherry flavoring, or more to taste

**Serves 4**

# Twisted Ice Cream Tiramisu

Line an 8" square baking pan with aluminum foil, leaving a 2" overhang on two opposite sides; spray with nonstick cooking spray. Arrange half the ladyfingers in the bottom of pan to cover; set aside. In a small bowl, stir together coffee and Kahlúa. Brush half of coffee mixture over ladyfingers in pan, allowing mixture to soak in. Stir coffee ice cream until smooth but not melted; spread over ladyfingers. Sprinkle half of grated chocolate over ice cream. Dollop 1½ cups whipped topping over chocolate and spread evenly. Place in freezer for at least 30 minutes or until firm.

To make second layer, soften dulce de leche ice cream in a medium bowl. Arrange remaining ladyfingers over whipped topping. Brush cookies with remaining coffee mixture. Stir caramel liqueur into softened ice cream and spread mixture over ladyfingers. Sprinkle remaining chocolate over ice cream. Dollop remaining whipped topping over chocolate layer and spread until smooth. Cover and freeze at least 3 hours or overnight.

Thirty minutes before serving, place dessert in refrigerator to soften slightly. Remove dessert from pan, peel off foil and cut into squares. Garnish with chocolate curls.

## You Will Need:

**Serves 9**

- 1½ (3.5 oz.) pkgs. ladyfingers (32 to 36 cookies)
- ¼ C. brewed coffee, room temperature
- ¼ C. Kahlúa (coffee liqueur)
- 1 pt. coffee ice cream, softened
- 3 (1 oz.) squares bittersweet chocolate, grated or finely chopped, divided
- 3 C. whipped topping, divided
- 1 pt. dulce de leche ice cream
- 1 T. caramel cream liqueur
- Milk chocolate curls, optional

# Bombsicle Ice

In a large measuring cup, mix blue raspberry vodka, corn syrup and lemonade concentrate. Divide crushed ice among serving dishes and pour an equal amount of vodka mixture over each. Serve immediately.

## You Will Need:

- ½ C. blue raspberry vodka
- ½ C. light corn syrup
- ¼ C. frozen lemonade concentrate
- 4 C. crushed ice

**Serves 4**

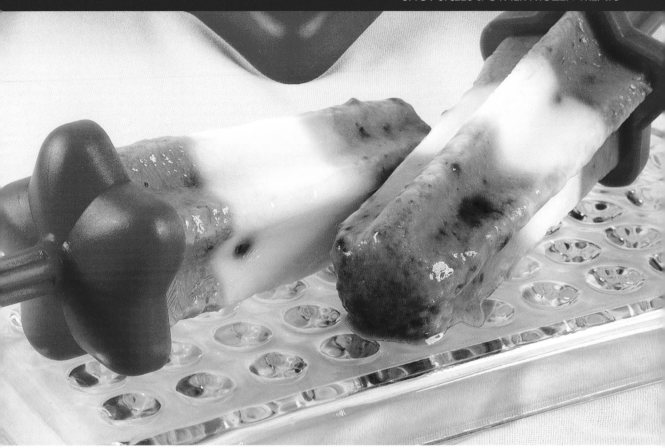

# Razzy Yo-Pops

In a medium bowl, mix yogurt and sugar. Place ¾
cup mixture in a blender. Add berries and raspberry
schnapps; blend well. Spoon alternating layers of berry
mixture and plain yogurt mixture into molds. Freeze 4
hours or until solid.

## You Will Need:

○ 2 C. plain low-fat yogurt
○ ½ C. sugar
○ ½ C. frozen raspberries
○ 2 T. raspberry schnapps

**Serves 6**

# Frozen Strawberry Margarita Pie

Preheat oven to 350°. Spray a 9" pie plate (4-cup capacity)* with nonstick cooking spray; set aside. In a medium bowl, stir together graham cracker crumbs, sugar and butter until well mixed. Press mixture evenly in the bottom and up the sides of prepared pie plate. Bake for 10 to 12 minutes or until slightly browned. Let cool in pan about 30 minutes.

Meanwhile, in a blender container, combine sliced strawberries, lime zest, lime juice, sweetened condensed milk, tequila and triple sec; puree until just smooth. Transfer to a large bowl. In a chilled mixing bowl with chilled beaters, beat whipping cream until it just holds stiff peaks. Gently fold ⅓ of whipped cream into strawberry mixture until blended. Then fold in remaining whipped cream. Pour filling into crust, mounding it slightly. Freeze 4 hours or until firm.

Before serving, remove pie from freezer and let soften in refrigerator about 40 minutes or until semi-soft. Cut into wedges. Garnish with sliced strawberries and limes, if desired.

* A 9" springform pan can be used. Press crumb mixture in the bottom and 1" up the sides of pan.

## You Will Need:

**Serves 8**

- ○ 1¼ C. graham cracker crumbs
- ○ 2 T. sugar
- ○ 5 T. butter, melted
- ○ 3½ C. sliced strawberries
- ○ 1 T. finely grated lime zest
- ○ ¼ C. lime juice
- ○ 1 (14 oz.) can sweetened condensed milk
- ○ 2 T. tequila
- ○ 2 T. triple sec
- ○ 1½ C. heavy whipping cream, chilled
- ○ Sliced strawberries and limes, optional

# Punchy Pops

In a medium bowl, mix punch and sweetened condensed milk until blended. Stir in lemon juice and gin. Pour into molds. Freeze at least 4 hours or overnight.

## You Will Need:

- 3 C. fruit punch
- 1 (14 oz.) can sweetened condensed milk
- 2 T. lemon juice
- ⅓ C. gin

**Serves 15**

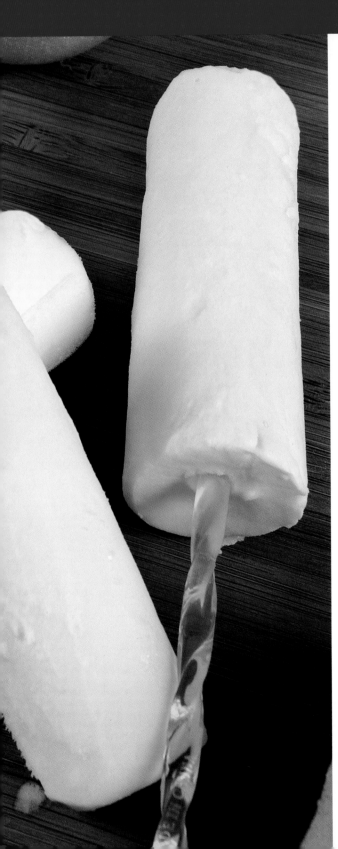

# Lemon-Rum Creamsicles

Using a vegetable peeler or sharp knife, remove rind from lemons in long strips. Squeeze juice from lemons to measure ²/₃ cup; set aside.

In a medium saucepan over medium heat, combine lemon rind, whipping cream, milk, sugar and salt, stirring occasionally until sugar is dissolved; simmer for 5 minutes. Remove from heat and let stand at room temperature for 20 minutes, stirring occasionally.

Slowly add reserved lemon juice to milk mixture, stirring constantly. Stir in citrus rum. Pour through a strainer into a large measuring cup, extracting as much liquid as possible; discard solids. Pour into molds; freeze overnight or until solid. Remove from molds, set on a tray and freeze again for several hours before serving.

## You Will Need:

- 3 to 4 fresh lemons
- 1 C. heavy whipping cream
- 1 C. milk
- ½ C. sugar
- ⅛ tsp. salt
- 2 T. citrus rum

**Serves 8**

## Serving Variation

Prepare mixture and pour into a bowl. Freeze overnight. Scoop into dishes and eat with a spoon.

# Kiwi Colada

In a small bowl, mix pineapple juice, cream of coconut and coconut rum. Pour into molds, filling halfway. Place two slices of kiwifruit in each mold against opposite sides. Fill with juice mixture and insert sticks between fruit. Freeze 3 hours or until solid.

## You Will Need:

- 1 (6 oz.) can pineapple juice
- 1 T. cream of coconut
- 2 tsp. coconut rum
- 1 to 2 kiwifruit, peeled and sliced

Serves
4

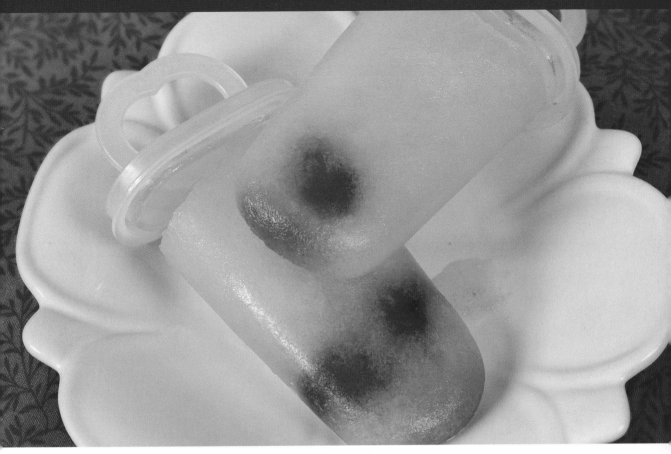

# OJ~Gin Pops

Drain cherries and pat dry; set aside. Sprinkle gelatin over juice and let stand for 1 to 2 minutes; mix well. Stir in gin. Place one or two cherries in each mold; pour juice mixture over cherries. Freeze overnight or until solid.

## You Will Need:

Serves 12

- 12 to 24 maraschino cherries
- 1 tsp. unflavored gelatin
- 4 C. orange juice
- ½ C. plus 2 T. gin

# Grasshopper

In a blender, combine ice cream, whipped topping, crème de menthe, crème de cacao and triple sec. Blend until smooth and thick. Pour into chilled glasses and sprinkle with cookie crumbs, if desired. Serve immediately.

**Serves 3**

## You Will Need:

- ○ 2 C. vanilla ice cream
- ○ ¾ C. whipped topping, thawed
- ○ 3 T. green crème de menthe
- ○ 2 T. crème de cacao
- ○ 1 T. triple sec
- ○ 1 chocolate cookie, crushed, optional

## Variations

Grasshopper Pops: In a blender, combine 4½ tablespoons green crème de menthe, 3½ tablespoons crème de cacao, 3 cups vanilla ice cream, 8 ice cubes and ¼ cup heavy whipping cream. Blend until smooth. Pour into molds and freeze overnight. To cover pops in chocolate, remove from molds; return to freezer for 30 minutes. Melt 1 cup chocolate candy wafers (or chocolate chips with 1 tablespoon shortening), stirring until smooth; let stand until cool but still liquid. Dip top half of pops in melted chocolate and quickly press tip into chocolate cookie crumbs, if desired. Return to freezer until serving time.

# White Russian Granita

In a medium saucepan over medium heat, mix sugar and 2¼ cups water until dissolved. Increase heat to high and bring to a boil. Remove from heat. Add coffee granules and stir to dissolve. Pour into a medium bowl and whisk in corn syrup, whipping cream, vodka and Kahlúa. Chill for 2 hours.

Transfer mixture to a shallow pan and freeze 3 hours, stirring occasionally. Cover and freeze overnight.

Thirty minutes before serving, set four cups in the freezer. Scrape the surface of granita with a fork and scoop into frosted cups. Serve immediately.

**Serves 4**

## You Will Need:

- ½ C. sugar
- 3 to 4 tsp. instant coffee granules
- 1 T. dark corn syrup
- ½ C. heavy whipping cream
- ¼ C. vodka
- ¼ C. Kahlúa

## Variations

Make White Russian in an ice cream maker by decreasing water by ½ cup and preparing as directed above. After refrigerating, transfer mixture to an ice cream maker and process according to manufacturer's directions. Transfer to a bowl, cover and freeze for 2 hours or until firm.

# Lime-Pear Sorbet

In a medium bowl, dissolve gelatin in 1 cup boiling water. Pour into a blender with soda, rum, lime juice and pears; blend until smooth. Pour mixture into a shallow pan. Freeze overnight, scraping with a fork occasionally. Mash and scoop into serving dishes. Serve promptly.

You Will Need:

- 1 (3 oz.) pkg. lime gelatin
- ¾ C. lemon-lime soda
- ¼ C. light rum
- 2 T. lime juice
- 1 (15.25 oz.) can pears, drained

Serves
6

# Brandy Slush

In a large bowl, dissolve sugar in 4½ cups boiling water; cool. Stir in lemonade and grape juice concentrates and blackberry brandy. Cover and freeze overnight; stir occasionally. Stir until slushy and spoon into glasses; serve immediately.

## You Will Need:

- ○ 1 C. sugar
- ○ ¾ C. frozen lemonade concentrate
- ○ ¾ C. frozen grape juice concentrate
- ○ 1 C. blackberry brandy

**Serves 8**

# Bombed Pops

In a large measuring cup, mix lemonade concentrate with 2 cans water. Divide mixture evenly between three smaller bowls, approximately 1½ cups per bowl. To one bowl, stir in Limoncello, grenadine and red food coloring. Pour red mixture into bottom third of molds and freeze 3 hours or until solid. Reserve remaining two bowls of lemonade.

To one of the reserved bowls of lemonade, stir in vodka. Pour white mixture over frozen red layer in molds, filling ⅔ full. Center a popsicle stick in each mold, fastening to hold sticks upright. Freeze 3 hours or until solid.

To remaining reserved bowl of lemonade, stir in blue curaçao and blue food coloring. Pour blue mixture over frozen white layer in molds until filled. Freeze overnight or until solid.

## You Will Need:

- 1 (12 oz.) can frozen lemonade concentrate, thawed
- 4 tsp. Limoncello
- 4 tsp. grenadine syrup
- 3 drops red food coloring
- 4 tsp. vodka
- 4 tsp. blue curaçao
- 4 drops blue food coloring

**Serves 12**

**Note**: For this recipe, avoid molds with stick/lid combination as sticks will be inserted partway through the freezing process.

# Blasted Berries

In a blender, combine cider, lemonade, raspberries, strawberries, raspberry sherbet, triple sec and rum. Blend until smooth. Pour into glasses and serve immediately.

## You Will Need:

- 1 C. apple cider
- 1½ C. lemonade
- 1 C. frozen raspberries
- 1 C. frozen strawberries
- 2 C. raspberry sherbet
- ¼ C. triple sec
- 2 T. light rum

**Serves 6**

Try freezing as ice cubes.

# Peppermint Shiver

In a blender, combine ice cream, crushed ice, milk, vodka, peppermint schnapps and peppermint extract. Blend until smooth and thick. Place in freezer while whipping the cream.

In a chilled mixing bowl with chilled beaters, beat whipping cream and red sugar until thick and pink. Beat in cinnamon schnapps until soft peaks form.

Spoon alternating layers of ice cream mixture and pink whipped cream into glasses and swirl lightly*. Garnish with whole or crushed candy canes. Serve immediately.

\* For a clear swirled effect, ice cream and whipped cream mixtures should be of similar thickness and consistency.

## You Will Need:

- O  2 C. vanilla ice cream
- O  ½ C. crushed ice
- O  2 T. milk
- O  1 T. vodka, chilled
- O  3 T. peppermint schnapps, chilled
- O  ½ tsp. peppermint extract
- O  ¾ C. heavy whipping cream
- O  1 T. red decorative sugar
- O  1¾ tsp. cinnamon schnapps
- O  Candy canes, whole and/or crushed

**Serves 4**

## ALCOHOL INGREDIENT INDEX

## RECIPES BY TITLE INDEX

# More Great Books from Fox Chapel Publishing

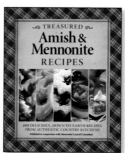
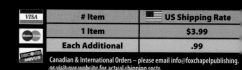